ST VA - YY

THE BUSINESS PLAN
APPROVED!

The Business Plan *Approved!*

VANDENBURGHS
Chartered Accountants

Gower

First published 1992 by Gower Publishing Company Limited, Aldershot, Hampshire

This paperback edition published 1994
Gower Publishing
Gower House
Croft Road
Aldershot
Hampshire GU11 3HR
England

Gower
Old Post Road
Brookfield
Vermont 05036
USA

CIP catalogue records for this book are available from the British Library

ISBN 0-566-07286-6 HBK
       0-566-07453-2 PBK

Phototypeset in 10pt Times by Intype, London
Printed and bound in Great Britain by
Hartnolls Limited, Bodmin, Cornwall

Contents

List of Tables

Introduction

'Good people will succeed in a venture even if their initial product is wrong.'

Business Planning is one of the few fundamental management techniques which is a prerequisite of running a successful business. Sometimes planning is done by accident and frequently it is done informally. It may be formalized at the demand of the bank or as a result of the need to raise equity funding or it may be the outcome of an internal review of the business. Regardless of how informal the planning process is, few businesses can survive without it; even fewer can fail to benefit from it. Planning is the art of choosing both where you want your business to go and how you think it will best get there.

During boom times, a Business Plan is viewed as being synonymous with raising equity, and in recession, with staving off the bank manager. Almost always, the term 'Business Plan' conjures up images of glossy documents with one goal in mind, that is, raising money. But at any time, a critical review of any business often reveals surprising weaknesses. The surprise is frequently related to how something very simple but important could have slipped through. This evaluation will almost always have a bearing on the glossy document. It may be that the sales points of the document are varied, or different aspects of the Plan are stressed. It may be that different ideas of growth are emphasized. Sometimes alternate ideas are created by the review. Sometimes, the ultimate objectives of the Plan are modified to reflect the current reality of the business. It is rare that a critical review can have anything other than a beneficial effect. This book is designed to improve the effectiveness of the process, to improve techniques for reviewing the business and to help present the better end results of the review to the bank, investor or employees. However, any business plan must be tailored to the specific circumstances of each company, and advice may be needed.

1

Part 1

First Steps to Planning

1   The Steps of an Effective Plan

'Deals which seem too good to be true rarely are – they are more likely to be inadequately thought out or simply unrealistic.'

When preparing a Business Plan, the first steps to be taken into account are:

1   Devising the Business Plan strategy
2   Costing the idea
3   Dealing with potential variations
4   Devising the Business Plan document
5   Establishing the objectives to formalize the Business Plan
6   Dealing with conflict between the strategy and the document

Gone are the days when the bank threw money at any company with a half-decent cash flow forecast and phantom security. Gone are the days when investors felt honoured to be given the opportunity to quadruple their investment overnight. Gone are the days when Managing Directors could run their businesses on a whim. The turn of the decade had heralded a far more sober evaluation of business potential. The nineties is the era of realism, a psychology that looks as if it will last at least into the mid-nineties. For today's environment, there is no longer room for businesses that are run in an unprofessional manner. Management must look ahead. It needs a clear Plan of where it is heading and how it will get there. The Plan must be open to proper scrutiny, and be convincing.

During the late eighties, companies were allowed to produce sloppy Plans. Bad practices became common as did the many misconceptions about the purpose and method of Plans. One of the most serious faults was the preparation of a 'glossy document' which lacked substance.

Another fault was the perception that Business Plans were only needed to raise

5

money. A weak company is in greater need of a Plan than a strong company. The purpose of the Plan is to review the company's activities. It must identify weak areas of the business and devise a Plan to eliminate those weaknesses. Equally it must identify the strong areas and encourage them. It must recognize or create new ideas and potential, and steer the company into a position to exploit those opportunities, if they can bring it closer to achieving its objectives. Only then should the business try raising funds, and even then, only if it needs to. In yesterday's market, Business Plans were the by-product of expansion. In today's, they will be seen as a function of consolidation of a business and good management.

There are four main stages to Business Planning:

1   Looking ahead to devise a Plan for the business over the short to medium term.
2   Working out how much funding the Plan needs and which form of funding is best (see Chapters 8 to 12).
3   Devising a Plan for dealing with any deviations that may occur during the time frame considered (see Chapters 13 to 14).
4   Documenting the conclusions to help achieve the Plans, and preparing a Business Plan document. This formalizes the Plan to banks, investors, shareholders, internal management and staff (see Chapters 4 to 7).

To increase the strength of the Plan, it is helpful to be clear about what is expected of it. It is therefore, worthwhile interviewing bankers, investors or other users (see Chapters 15 to 18).

Devising the Business Plan Strategy

The first part of the Planning process needs a sound knowledge of what is happening in the business. The company's objectives must be clearly evaluated and the degree to which the company is currently achieving those objectives needs to be judged. The skill of the entrepreneur is to understand the company's strengths and weaknesses. The successful entrepreneur will create ways of eliminating the weak areas and recognize, create and exploit opportunities and strengths. This book assumes you have identified your company's strengths and weaknesses and that you have ideas on how to improve the company. Unfortunately, with too many businesses, this is where the planning ends. In order to plan properly, this is where the planning should begin.

There are many ideas for strengthening a company: improve the sales force; develop new products; soften the product's image to attract more customers; spend more; spend less. But, for every idea, there are costs. Adding to the sales force (or to any other resource) has direct costs. Reducing the advertising budget cuts at the foundation of the sales effort and, in turn, depletes revenue. The trick is to manage activities so that new income exceeds its cost. This will always be more successful when planned.

Costing the Idea

The first step in the planning process involves creating a strategy. The second projects what the effect of the Plan is most likely to be. New revenues are forecast. Actions needed to generate any additional income are considered in turn, and the cost of each is estimated. The net results suggest how successful the ideas may be. Sometimes the results are surprising, other times they prove exactly what was expected. The mechanics of the Profits Plan is dealt with in Chapters 9 and 10, to help ensure expectations are not artificially high.

The next target in this step is an integral part of any Plan. It deals with how much funding is likely to be needed. It costs money to implement new ideas. The direct costs are often obvious. Buying assets and allocating a marketing budget, for example, are easily seen and accurately quantified. The indirect costs are often more subtle. The benefits of growing are not reaped until there has been time for the changes to have an effect. Any regular increased costs, such as salaries, are spent and need to be funded until new revenues cover the extra costs. In addition, as a business develops, so does its need for space and investment. The value of stock and debtors usually rises beyond the ability of the business to delay payments to its suppliers. This working capital growth needs funding in exactly the same way as the cost of extra investment. Many of these costs can easily be overlooked.

When the costs of ideas are small, few businesses have difficulty in funding them. The indirect costs tend to be limited to the interest of additional borrowings and the non-financial costs of ideas, such as possible motivational and perceptional problems. But once the ideas have become substantial, they invariably cost more and require more funding. No business has unlimited funding and it is very likely the additional funding needs of new ideas will divert some cash from other areas of the business. This may reduce the effectiveness of those particular areas or, at least, restrict their ability to develop their own ideas for a while. In addition, the lost profits from the redirecting is as much a development cost as paying for, say, a new salesman. While indirect funding and cost flows of development can be difficult to see, quantifying their future values is all but impossible. (See Chapters 11 and 12 for further discussion on funding.)

Dealing with Potential Variations

The third part of the strategy explores methods of dealing with risk. Quite apart from the difficulties of quantifying how well the business ideas will work, there is the added problem of dealing with the consequences of the actual results deviating from the anticipations, once the Plan has been implemented.

Regardless of how much funding is needed to set the Plan in motion, additional funds are needed to cover every shortfall. The planner must evaluate the likelihood of shortfall and by how much the Plan might fail. This must be put in perspective according to the amount of overall funding available to the business and the consequences of how well the original Plan will be able to succeed if the extra funds required cannot be found. This needs the Planner to deal with the effect of benefits taking longer to accrue than estimated, and the monetary effect of benefits being less, or costs being more, than forecast. It requires consideration of the effects on all aspects of the business. Developing any one area of business almost always has an indirect effect on other areas.

In short, Business Planning demands complex evaluations, and the process often requires tailoring and may point to alternate solutions for growth. Examples of the type of areas reviewed include considering different sales prices and re-evaluating debt collection and discount policies. Some target markets may be dropped and others expanded. The importance of dealing with risk is chillingly emphasized by one Bank Manager we spoke to who believes that 30% of the growth Plans he has seen fail have done so for lack of arranging an adequate 'escape' route in the event that forecasts were excessive.

Devising the Business Plan Document

Preparing the Business Plan document is the final part of the Planning process. It can be aimed at several different people. The person at whom it is aimed will determine its contents. One of the most important groups of people at whom the document is aimed is the company's staff. Setting out a formal Plan gives a clear and unequivocal message to management and staff about what is expected. It is generally accepted that if the management and staff of a company know what they are expected to do, they are more likely to be able to achieve it.

Another function of the document is to raise funds, usually from a bank or from an investor. As a kickback from the late eighties, the start point is that the readers will disbelieve the numbers. Rob Pike of National Westminster Bank expressed sentiment succinctly when he said 'I always view the numbers with a good helping of scepticism'. To deal with this problem, it is important to understand why he, and almost all other Business Plan users who were interviewed, are not being bloody-minded when they say they disbelieve what they are shown. There are two key factors to take into account. First, it is not easy to get the figures right. There are so many factors – external to the organization – which affect the company's ability to succeed; all Plans are vulnerable to failure. Secondly, almost all of the readers have seen so many Plans which have failed that they have an instinctive scepticism about what they are shown. Thirdly, a good number of Business Plan authors have a blind belief in the success of the products and ability. Whereas it is not necessarily unfounded, it is often better for both parties if the banker or investor takes the opposite view. It allows them to test out the robustness of the Plan and the resilience of the individuals involved.

Objectives of the Business Plan

Despite the practical problems, the primary aim of a Business Plan is to formalize new ideas. The first three stages of the planning process are vital to secure the most appropriate route for the company. By undertaking the whole series of analyses to see the effect on profits and funding of failure and alternative options, the planner can arrange contingency action and funding if necessary.

One benefit is that the Plan provides an 'early warning' system of potential failure by having clear targets that should be met. If the early figures show adverse trends, there is the opportunity for management to react to reverse the trends. With clear criteria for judging success, management can know when it must spend time fine tuning activities, which directly improves the chances of achieving success.

The secondary aim of the Plan is almost as vital as the first. It must persuade those who instinctively disbelieve Business Plans that they should put their money into your business. They are not benevolent, so you need to convince them to invest in your business as opposed to someone else's. This means that the Plan must convince them that their money is less at risk and will earn more if they invest in or lend to your business instead of in, say, a bank deposit or to one of your competitors. The power of persuasion is an art in itself and several books deal exclusively with that subject. However, there are comments throughout this book which should give you insight into the thought processes of a Business Plan user. These comments can be a useful guide as to what you should and should not say in a Plan to ensure it is read to your best advantage. One of the strongest aids to persuasion is having the right product (or Plan) at the right price (or return to the lender/investor). (See Chapters 4 to 7.)

Before embarking on drafting any Plan document, it pays to be aware of a couple of interesting features which motivate Business Plan readers. Readers are just as concerned to see how safe their money will be in the event that the Plan is not met as about how much money they can make if the operations succeed. They also believe that it is crucial for a business to develop a coherent and accurate Plan and to follow that Plan closely. Therefore, that Plan must be able to cope with all eventualities.

Dealing with Conflict between the Strategy and the Document

Business Planning has two components, two goals. One is the creation of an internal Plan, the other is the presentation of the Plan to external users. Unfortunately, however, they conflict.

To persuade an investor, the Plan must convey a positive message, showing the likely rate of return on the investment. A banker wants reassurance on the ability of the company to repay the money to the bank without the bank needing to take undue risk. The return the bank is looking for is, accordingly, far lower – just the rate of interest plus one or two per cent profit margin. It is the document's job to convince the banker or investor. On the other hand, as a business tool, you are using it to deal with uncertainty, exactly the thing that turns bankers and investors off.

In reality, investors know full well about the risks involved. They tend to worry more about the risk of missing the market. Bankers tend to be more concerned with adequate security for their loan. As a business tool, the Plan puts a higher priority on dealing with the practical and operational problems of missing targets. If the final Plan deals too much with potential practical problems, it will detract from the bigger picture. If it doesn't deal with them enough, the Plan will be perceived to be ill-conceived. The solution to this conflict is to deal with the Plan in two parts. The document aimed at bankers or investors contains most of the analytical review of the business, its growth plans and the rewards of investing. The investor wants to understand the 'market driven' risks. (See Chapters 4 and 5.) A series of financial models should be prepared which deal with all financial aspects of the Plan. These incorporate the expected outcome and also the likely effect of failing to meet or exceeding targets. The business evaluation of the likelihood of each alteration, compared with the financial effect, occurs before the final document is in place. This evaluation would be available to investors, and particularly bankers, who have decided the Plan is worth looking into further. It does not, however, have to be thrust down their throat at the outset. The Business Plan document is, therefore, a summary of certain parts of the models, together with an analysis of the business environment. The financial models are, however, as integral to the overall Business Plan as the Plan document itself. Since this book is devoted to the Business Plan as a whole, the restricted document aimed at bankers and investors is clearly distinguished where appropriate.

Chapter Summary

- There are four steps to Business Planning. A strategy is devised, it is costed, the possibility of missing targets is looked at and the strategy is modified or changed, if it is worthwhile. Then finally, the ideas are formalized into a document. This Business Plan document can be aimed at investors, bankers, directors, managers or staff.
- There are two primary objectives of preparing the document. The first is to formalize your ideas. This provides a benchmark against which to judge how well the business is doing in the future. The second is to persuade bankers or investors to back the Plan, and to help motivate staff to work in the right direction.
- There is a conflict between carrying out the planning process for yourself and preparing the Business Plan document for others. This conflict is best resolved by divorcing the two processes, preparing the document only after the strategy evaluation is complete.

2 Who Should Prepare the Plan

'If I see a Plan with the auditor's name on the front, I will not even bother to read it. I want to see what management want, not their advisors.'

One word of caution about preparing a Business Plan! Make sure the right people are involved in its preparation. Some people write the Plan with minimum reference to the Financial Directors or financial advisors. Some Plans are written exclusively by the outsiders. Most non-financial directors believe a Business Plan is limited to a sales document to raise funds. It is too easy to omit integrating the ideas for growth with both direct and indirect costs arising from carrying out those ideas. It is even easier to fail to set aside funds to cater for the consequences of their plans going awry. As a result, the non-financial Plan often lacks reality and is prone to failure at the first obstacle.

Conversely, many organizations perceive the Business Plan to be a purely financial exercise for others. They delegate full responsibility for preparation of the Plan exclusively to the Financial Directors or their advisors. In common with their co-Directors, many Financial Directors think of a Business Plan as a numerical exercise to quantify the financial effect of ideas of the business entrepreneurs. They will often ignore, or be asked to ignore, the business and practical side of implementing Plans. The result is a financial forecast which does not reflect all cost consequences of changing direction. It is almost impossible for them to have any real grasp on the likelihood of the Plan failing or the extent of possible shortfalls from targets. This prevents them from providing a realistic, or for that matter useful, Plan and it is consequently given a low priority by the rest of the management team.

The moral of the story is that Plans are far better, more realistic and useful, if prepared by a team of those having responsibility for various parts of the business. And the better the Plan, the better are its chances of success. If handled properly, joint involvement can also create a tremendous motivational spirit throughout the organization.

Some companies delegate the entire documentation process to external advisors or consultants. Whereas the content of the document is likely to be complete, it is usually too analytical for the reader to 'feel' for the business. None of the enthusiasm for the product is there, which makes the Plan boring or 'sterile', as one investment manager complains. Although this is a very practical point, consider how much more likely the reader is to have a positive reaction to the Plan if he does not dread turning the page in case of finding another unyielding wall of numbers and facts. It is very important that all management is involved in the document. And if you feel enthusiastic about your company, enthuse. It makes for a far more interesting read.

3   Understanding Why the Business Plan Document Works

'Business Plans often aren't worth the paper they are written on. They are not convincing.'

The early nineties are proving tough. Throughout the economy, business is failing to meet targets; banks are discovering unpaid loans; investors are finding the return on their investments falling well below the rates of interest banks are paying out. These circumstances are not conducive to encourage risk taking. One of the prime goals for business is to consolidate. Profitable parts of the business must be preserved – unprofitable parts must be shelved or reorganized.

Even during the boom years of the eighties, Christopher Curry of the Piper Trust investment fund, along with many others, was claiming he had rarely seen a Business Plan's forecasts being achieved. There is a climate of historically excessive optimism in virtually all Business Plans and banks and investors experienced considerable losses during the depths of the recession. The task of convincing them is difficult.

There are two aspects of the Business Plan. One is the Plan for development of the Business (see Chapters 9 to 15). The other is the document which embodies the main conclusions of the Plan in a document aimed at banks and investors, which is intended to persuade them to participate in the Plan and is the subject of this chapter.

Objective of the Plan

When you explain how profitable a business is, the point is made by stating profits. When you explain how effective the personnel of an organization are, the point is more subjective and it is more difficult to prove. You may include a description of relevant experience, productivity or staff turnover. When you explain how strong a Business

Plan is, the point is almost exclusively subjective. Proof involves a lot of description. There are good ways and bad of doing this.

Keith Davies of National Westminster Bank complains that many businesses seem to prepare the Business Plan document for their own use. It is all too common for them to perceive the readers of a Business Plan to be simple or inexperienced. Bank managers may not have had much experience at running a business themselves, but almost all will have had a great amount of experience at reading Plans and comparing the actual outcomes with projected figures. Indeed they may look at a couple of hundred each year. If they have a weak understanding about your specific business, that will be to your disadvantage. People who are unsure will act far more cautiously than those with a thorough understanding of the business. It is therefore your job to explain the relevant aspects of your business in order to give them the specific understanding that they need to be able to be of most help. But it is a mistake to conclude that, because someone does not fully understand the specifics of your business, they could not understand general business principles. Similarly, any investor will not risk money in a business without being very clear about the potential rewards as well as the risks.

The most effective way to prove the strength of a Business Plan is analogous to a description of the efficiency of a chosen route when travelling to a designated town.

The Analogy

A sales department is required to justify to you the best way for you to travel to a customer. The criteria for judging the effectiveness is the cost of getting there. The cost depends on the distance travelled (petrol, the direct cost of travel) and the time of the journey (wages, the indirect cost of the journey). To be convinced, you would want to see a map of where the journey started and where the customer was. You would want to see whether the proposed route would take the car to the correct place. You would then look at the alternate routes. Once the ground rules have been laid, the job of convincing starts.

The criteria for selecting one route over another will depend on the time taken to travel along each road and the cost. The extra cost from obstacles would be taken into account. If road works or traffic jams are known about, these are incorporated into the computation. Then the difficult part, the risk of unknown obstacles. The risk is that there may be road works or traffic of which no-one has direct knowledge. You would take more account of advice from people who had driven down these roads many times before, but less account of advice from people who had driven down the roads only once or twice. You would put low weighting on help from people who had spoken to drivers, but this weighting would vary according to who had been spoken to and who had been asking. At the bottom end of the scale would be advice from anyone who could not show you that they knew the ground rules, had experience, or knew the obstacles.

The method to convince a bank or investor to back a Plan is surprisingly similar.

Structure of the Business Plan

For reasons more easily understood from the analogy, the Business Plan is structured in a conventional format. It first sets out the Current Activities of the company. It sets out where the company has been and where it is now, by describing the company and by summarizing key features of previous accounts. It then sets out what the Target is and how it will be achieved. This is the core of the Plan and is probably the most important part of the document. The final stage deals with risk – in particular the obstacles to development. This stage is subtle and is integrated into other sections. The Plan must provide as strong an argument as possible that all potential hazards have been identified together with the risk of failure. It must show that the risk of failure is low. You would explain your choice of how you intend to develop the company to give reassurance to someone who is looking to inject money into your business.

Before looking at the detail of how it should be done, there are a couple of things that must not be done. There is little that is less inspiring to an investor than reading a Plan which backtracks, fails properly to show the growth route or shows more than one route. Such a Plan indicates poor Planning which is a sign of bad management. No-one invests in a company if they think the management is bad. The Plan must not, therefore, be disorganized.

If the ground work has not been done, it is painfully apparent when reading a Business Plan. When writing the Plan, it is tempting to short-cut the earlier Planning stages if available time is sparse. The result gives an impression of superficiality – another common reason for rejection. The document must wait until after the basic Plan is shown to be sound.

Chapter Summary

- The main purpose of the Business Plan document is to explain to the reader the business you are in and your business strategy for the next three years or so.
- The best way of explaining this is analogous to giving road map directions for a journey. You need to explain where you are, where you are going and how you intend to get there.
- The document must be well structured. Firstly it must set out the Current Activities of the business. Then it must describe both the Target of the business, and how the target will be achieved. Finally you must explain how well the business can cope if the targets are not met in full.

Part 2

Contents of the Business Plan Document

4 Describing the Company

'A Business Plan must have a logical flow. It must contain all the information I am looking for. If it lacks a description on competition, for example, I will not read it any further. It is the only way I have of judging whether management are well organized and able to communicate. If not, they are unlikely to be able to run a business well.'

The conventionally accepted way to explain the present position of a business, is to describe in sections: Main activities, Company history, Position within the industry, Market analysis and Competition.

The reason behind the structure of the Business Plan document is important to understand. It helps to improve the contents of each section since it provides insight into what people are looking for when they are reading it (see Chapter 15 for investors' views, Chapter 16 for bankers', Chapter 17 for lawyers' and Chapter 18 for accountants').

From the Plan, its readers expect to establish firstly where the company is at the moment and where you are going, and secondly, they want to see how you are going to get there. This chapter deals with how to show the most flattering picture of where you are. Chapters 19 to 21 give worked examples of how organizations put into practice the sections described below and it may be helpful to refer to them whilst reading this chapter.

Put yourself in the position of your reader. Imagine you have plenty of money at your disposal. You have been commissioned to safeguard that money. You know you can deposit it in a long-term deposit account, guaranteeing a reasonable rate of interest, with almost no chance of losing the original money. Imagine someone you have never met before sends you some papers with an offer: let them have your money and you may get back more than you would by leaving your money in a bank account. But if things don't go quite right, you could lose more than just the interest you would have received. You could also lose the original capital. Needless to say, you would want to be very convinced. Now, add into the picture another nineteen Plans with their requests and offers. You are now in the position of your reader. Obviously, this is a highly competitive position to be in. You are about to give the reader a very important first impression of the business, so how do you describe it?

Main Activities

Provide a brief description about what you do. It is important not to be excessive in length or self-praise. It is also important to infuse any excitement you feel about the business into the description. Describe your products or services and the needs that they satisfy. If there is any reason why your products are unique or strong, the features should be described and explained. If there are any patents or licences held by the company, these should be briefly mentioned. If there is any natural development for the company's products or services which will provide future growth, the circumstances and potential should be set out here.

Describe the nature of your main customers and suppliers. If relevant, give details of the regions in which both operate. Give a little information about key personnel, if beneficial.

You should include your business philosophy, if you have one. This includes a description of how the company's products were chosen and developed and what the company's marketing strategy is.

Remember, this is the first impression. It should be as concise and interesting as possible. You want to draw the reader into the Plan. Many readers claim they make up their minds within the first five minutes of looking at a Plan. So make it punchy.

Company History

This section should set out the company's performance over the last three to five years. In numeric terms, the history should show Turnover, Gross Profits, total overheads and net profits. It should also show the company's asset position in summary. There should be a descriptive analysis setting out the company's development into its main areas of activity. If the company has had any setbacks during the past five years, these should also be explained, along with any reasons why these are not expected to recur.

The information should be presented for easy reading. Detail should only be incorporated if it substantially assists the reader to interpret the results. If the trends have been affected by an abnormal occurrence, explicitly state how and why the trend was affected. But providing too much detail will detract from this background information.

Position within your Industry

This section states the size of your business relative to the industry in which you operate. You need to describe your size and niche – what you do in particular that distinguishes you from your competition. You need to establish how much of your business is affected by the performance of your competitors and how much depends on development of the size of markets within the industry as a whole. This is one of the most crucial areas of the Plan as far as most investors are concerned, being one of the key risk areas. It provides a benchmark by which to judge how realistic the aspirations for turnover are. It also gives some indication about obstacles to the planned business route by describing competition. Because it is so crucial, it is divided into two parts.

Market analysis

Part one sets out the Market Analysis; the market size and its historic movements. It incorporates the company's share of the market with a historic perspective. Its narrative explains the markets by defining the activities included within each market. The market can be divided geographically, by product, by consumer, by value of product or many other appropriate ways. The main purpose is to define the size of potential turnover the company could achieve if it were to win 100% of the market. The purpose of setting out comparisons with the previous years is to establish the trend. This allows projection of the market size over the next few years. If there are any factors resulting in a market size which is likely to differ from a normal 'projection' of past trends, these should be clearly stated. It is clearer to state your expectations of the market size, explicitly, if you have any clear views.

If there are any factors that affect the industry, these should be explained. If population trends or regulatory developments impact on the industry, you should explain the development and effect.

This section establishes a platform of credibility for the Plan, and therefore the following factors should be carefully observed:

- Obtain accurate figures, and state where those figures are obtained from.
- If there are likely to be any unusual developments in the market, show any authority you have for these conclusions.
- Do not exceed three sentences in your description of any topic, unless absolutely vital.

Competition

Part two provides details of the competition. One professional investor says that he would immediately dismiss a Plan if it did not refer to competition. The purpose is to allow the reader to judge how intense competition is and how well you are likely to cope with it, and it with you. This section should include the names, sizes and profitability of the main parties in the industry. A brief description of any distinguishing feature of each competitor would be helpful and a general statement about the climate of competition is usually well received. Remember, competition to one person is a risk, to another it is an opportunity. But failure to evaluate the competitive nature of your industry is likely to worry a reader who is likely to fear the worst, in the absence of any opposite view being shown. If any competitors have recently entered or left the industry, the reasons should be explained.

If relevant, the strengths and weaknesses of your competitors' financial positions and managerial skills should be evaluated. If any competitors are doing particularly well or badly, the reasons should be established and explained. The reader is looking to see whether you are able to see strengths and weaknesses in the industry, since that is the start point for your being able to exploit opportunities and deal with your own weaknesses.

There are certain industries where market sizes are so large and with so much competition, that no one company or group comes even close to being dominant. For companies in these industries, describing specific competitors is less important. What is important, however, is to use this section to show how your products or services fit in with or are distinguished from the rest of the industry.

Ensure any competitive edge you have over competitors is clearly highlighted. If being smaller than competitors is better, say so. If being bigger is better, say so. The description of each competitor should not exceed one paragraph of five lines each, unless there is some compelling reason otherwise.

Chapter Summary

- The Current Activities of the business must be explained by setting out the main activities, the company history, a description of the market in which the company operates and the position of the business relative to competitors.
- The section describing the Main Activities should contain a brief description of what the business does.
- The section describing the Company History should set out the trading results of the company over the last few years. It should also describe the trends and explain any unusual variations.
- The section describing the position of the business must analyse the marketplace, how the market has developed and how the market will be developing over the period of the Plan. The section should also analyse how your company fares relative to your competitors.

5 The Target

'I want to know as soon as possible what the requirements of the business are. I want an overview of what the deal is. Then the Plan must lead on to prove to me how the business will succeed; how it will achieve its target.'

The section explaining the plan's target should describe: what the target is; how the target will be achieved – the strategy; and the summary.

The Target

In many respects, this is the easy part. The final target is the last thing to describe in a Business Plan. To get here, all the hard work of selecting the most appropriate growth plan must have been finished and all the numbers must have been calculated.

The target is stated in terms of profits and funding expected over the next three to five years. The section sets out the profits that are targeted by the business and how much profit is expected. It establishes the market share being targeted, which defines the level of turnover planned. If the company is planning to change its market share, the method of achieving the change must be explained. If no change is expected, say so. No change is considered far more achievable and less risky than proposing growth.

The target should be concise and simple. It should detail the projected profits from each area of activity and the required funding. If the Plan is aimed at an investor, it should specify the expected rate of return on the investment. The section should contain a summary of expected trading results. The detailed sales, gross profit, net profit and cash flow forecasts should be relegated to appendices.

Projections should go forward only as far as would be helpful to demonstrate the point you are trying to make. If you are raising equity, you would probably forecast figures for a three- to five-year period. It is common to show monthly forecasts for the first year, then quarterly thereafter. To support a request for a short-term bank over-draft, however, it is likely that the forecasting results over the next year would suffice.

If the numbers have not been constructed properly, as described in Chapters 8 to 14, it will be apparent. This stage is short in the Plan, but must not be included without proper preparation.

Description of How the Target will be Achieved – the Strategy

This is the 'crunch' section in the Plan. It describes the method selected to achieve growth. It is the basis on which the reader can evaluate the likelihood of growth. If this part is weak, readers will conclude the Plan is poor, regardless of how glossy your report is or how fervently you believe in your growth potential.

It is difficult to generalize about how the Plan should aim to achieve the growth, since there are so many different possibilities. Calculating the costs of your ideas is explained in Chapters 8 to 10. Selecting the best ideas is dealt with in Chapters 13 and 14. Remember, though, that this section of the Plan should not contain any of these speculations. Having selected the Plan, the document must be confident and unwaivering. It should describe the method chosen. Any variations or descriptions of how the Plan was selected can be discussed with the investor once your Plan has been considered worthy of further investigation.

The Target section must set out clearly the key aspects of the Plan. The key reasons for adopting the Plan should be set out clearly in order to illustrate the strength of the Plan and the likelihood of achieving the Target. The pricing and marketing plan must be explained briefly. If you have chosen to undercut the price of competitors, for example, the extent and rationale should be explained. The justification of the choice also needs to be explained. If prices are set at a higher level than the average, the extra benefits of the product must be clear and how the marketing strategy seeks to distinguish these additional benefits should be set out. Any reasons for believing that these benefits are worth the extra price and that customers will pay the extra, must be emphasized.

If the Plan bases the business on recent performance, it has the strength of being verifiable. If there are any developments away from historic performance, there is an added risk dimension. In these cases, the Plan needs to be even more convincing and should be properly researched. If new products have been developed, potential cus-tomers should be contacted and their interest levels summarized. Market research should be carried out, whether by a formal instruction to a market research company to act, or by informal contact with customers or potential customers. If there is any question about whether a new product is technically capable of performing, details of research or evidence of testing should be summarized. The more money that is needed to fund development, the stronger the research should be.

If the company has any key customers, the size and nature of the customer should be specified, together with any other information that may be relevant to help establish what will happen to demand from that customer in future. The same applies if demand comes from a key industry rather than from a key customer. This may be dealt with in the Current Activities section.

If the company needs to develop outside its present premises, the reasons and proposals should be explained. If helpful, the company's current location and facilities should be described.

The company's operational strategy should be explained. If the company plans to manufacture or subcontract its production, brief details along with any reasons for the choice should be given. If the company is a service industry, details of the company's employment, training and control policies for the next few years should be provided. For both goods and service industries, the company's quality control procedures should be outlined.

The policy of control of assets and liabilities should be described, as should the reasons for Inventory levels. If there are significant levels of Fixed Assets, the benefits should be expounded. The company's policy towards debtor levels and liabilities should be integrated with any other aspects that may be key to the business. If discount policies encourage early payment, for example, this may, if relevant, be connected with policies on the company's margins and industry positioning.

Any other operational factors or plans which you believe are at the heart of the company's success should be described. These may include the company's research and development policy, sales distribution policy, supply policy and personnel policy.

For an investor, this section represents the pillar of the Plan. It must be clear and concise. No other single part of the Plan will persuade or dissuade more than this. Credibility of any Plan to develop the company is vital. Any information that can be given to provide substance for the Plan should be stated. If you feel enthusiastic about the Plan, there is no prize for suppressing it. If your Plan has energy, it is likely to be more appealing to the reader.

The Summary of the Plan

There is no more important section in the Plan than the summary section. It is positioned at the very beginning and is thus the first thing to be read. It must therefore be punchy and concise. It must include all the relevant features of the Plan. In fact, many users have expressed that they reject Plans purely on the strength that the Summary is too weak or boring.

The Summary must show, on one page, what the company does and what its financial history has been. It must describe what the company's industry is and where the industry is going. It must set out the target for the company and how the company intends to achieve that target. It must state how much funding is needed, what the funds are for, and how much the company is prepared to pay for those funds.

Do not start this section until the Plan has been completed. Spend more time on this section than any other. Add in enthusiasm and excitement. Lighten up the page with pictures or attach a brochure to the Plan to give the reader a feel for the product. Be clear that this is where many of the Plans succeed or fail.

Summary

- The Target section of the document must clearly set out the target. This should be stated in terms of both the expected profits planned and the expected funding needed to achieve those profits.
- Describing how the target will be achieved is the core of the document. The Strategy section must therefore set out the method selected to achieve the target. It should itemize the key components of the method and explain why that method was selected.
- The Plan needs to be summarized. The Summary gives an easily digestible understanding of the Plan. It is effective only if it gives the reader a quick and clear understanding without reading the detail. This must go at the front of the document and summarize the key aspects of its contents. This gives readers their first impression of you. It should be punchy, using the style that will most impress.

6 Funding Requirements

'Too many businesses fail because they are not properly financed. It is tragic.'

If the market analysis is the key to an investor's heart, the cash flow forecast is the joy of the bank. It is worth bearing this in mind when setting out the funding requirements of the Plan.

This is best structured by preparing a cash flow forecast as an appendix and describing the key uses to which any additional funding will be put in the body of the Plan. Any assets the company has which are available to a bank for security should be summarized here. The more risky the Plan, the better the security will need to be.

For the investor, you should provide the expected rate of return on the investment. Clarify the equity sought and the share of the company being allocated. Then set out the projected value of the share at the end of the projection. The rate of return can be calculated by comparing the future value with the original cash injection. This is a potentially complex subject since it involves future valuations and compounding rates over the life of the investment. Professional advice should be taken on which numbers to show.

An investor who will own less than 50% of the company will be concerned with how the investment can be realized. This is another area in which professional advice can be valuable. If a solution is proposed, such as an intention to 'go public', the possibility should be expressed.

The structure of required funding should also be described in this section, together with any reasoning that may be relevant to the reader. (See Chapter 12.)

Imagine you were asked to lend a sum of money equal to the size of loan you are asking for from the Bank to a friend. Read your Plan and see if you are convinced you will get your money back, with interest. Then consider whether you would prefer to lend the same money to one of the other nineteen Plans you were reading. Now, with

27

some feeling for what the Bank manager is thinking, read your Plan once again to see how important the security is. Only proceed if you are still happy with this section.

7 Dealing With Risk

'If management do not have experience, that does not automatically kill the deal. But the Bank wants to know who the people are. We assume they don't have the experience if they do not say they do.'

There are also two other factors which must be addressed: Management and Sensitivity Analysis.

The ground rules of the Plan have been established, the Target defined and the method of achieving the Target set out. The final piece to the Business Plan jigsaw is Risk.

There is rarely a section in a document specifically allocated to Risk. There are several reasons for this, one of which is that you do not want to draw attention to the potential problems before your reader has had a chance to digest the potential rewards of lending or investing in your business.

Some of the most important questions a reader will have in mind are: How likely is the Plan to succeed? What chance is there of improving on the Plan? How much risk is there that the Plan will fall below target and how much could be lost? How does this combination of potential return, likelihood of return, potential amount to lose and likelihood of loss, compare with other Plans? And how does this all compare with putting the money into a bank deposit?

Some of these 'risk' type questions are dealt with in the sections on Current Activities and the Target. Some specific obstacles to achieving targets are dealt with in the analysis of the market size and competition. This particular chapter, however, describes how the Plan covers others aspects of Risk, without sticking up a flag with a skull and cross-bones on it, and stating 'Now read this!'.

Management

One major factor of Risk which has not yet been dealt with is the risk of management not having the experience or ability to make the Plan work. Two fundamental problems are often caused if management lacks experience. Firstly, they are unlikely to judge well how much turnover can be attained in practice and secondly, they are unlikely to know the true costs of running the organization at the projected level of activities. A section describing the background of management is, therefore, always expected.

The management team should be described. The bank manager often knows the management team, but the manager's Head Office is less likely to do so. The investor often does not. The purpose of the description is to give the reader a feel of how well experienced the management team is. Any relevant experience the management has should be brought out in this section. Surprisingly, a weakness in management is not always a problem. Some fund managers would prefer to know that management weakness had been identified and accepted since the gap can be filled by recruitment, if necessary. The important points to bring out are the relevant backgrounds that give the management team the experience to run the planned business, and also the success that has been achieved to demonstrate your management capabilities. More than that is irrelevant and likely to irritate or bore the reader.

Sensitivity Analysis

So far, dealing with risk has involved presentation of the circumstances that indicate how likely it is that the projections can be achieved. The final coverage of risk sets out the effect on profits and cash flow of failing to achieve targets. This becomes more important where the risk of failure is perceived to be high.

The purpose of this analysis is to show whether the business can succeed even in poorer times and to satisfy a lender or investor that their money will not be lost if their worst fears are realized – that gross profits will be lower or costs higher than forecast. They are not interested in the numeric effect of specific failure. Rather, they are interested in what actions will be taken to safeguard their money in the event of specific failures.

The sensitivity analysis is a demonstration of the cash and profit effect of diverging from the Plan in specific respects. Dealing with sensitivity analysis should be done sensitively. Excessive analysis is boring and may detract from the main impact of the Plan. However, Risk must be dealt with. It is often dealt with in conceptual terms in the Target section, by identifying the strength of the Plan. However, to the extent that contingency funding is sought, brief details should be mentioned. Although the Plan should not include excessive contingency type numbers, the calculations must have been carried out.

Part 3

Devising the Plan

8 Introduction

'No one can do any better than attempt at a forecast. No one can predict what will happen in the future. But the forecast is a benchmark against which to highlight problems at an early stage. Without them, I can be sure a business is not being managed properly.'

When Margaret Thatcher came to power, she had enormous and expansive visions about how to develop the nation. She did not have a plan to expand the country with any direct action. Instead she intended to create an environment within which industry would flourish. She wanted to reduce artificial barriers to trade. She promoted free competition and old-fashioned work ethics. During her reign, there was almost as much controversy about her methods as there was about whether the plans were, in fact, succeeding.

As a result, the early eighties saw a mighty recession designed to 'cleanse' the economy of dead wood, lame ducks and inefficient industry. There is no doubt that the economy grew and became wealthier than ever before. The effect of this short-term gain will be a lasting one. It may, as intended, have created an efficient base from which the economy will flourish. Or conversely, it may have decimated forever the manufacturing base of the economy. Computing the net effect of the Thatcher era is complex. The final analysis of its success will probably depend on the political inclination of the evaluator. But everyone will agree that many features must go into the equation, which means that there are many positive as well as negative aspects to establishing how successful the plan was. Only after this evaluation will historians conclude whether her plan was right at the time.

Objectives of the Plan

When preparing any plan, from a simple planned road map to the immensely complex 'economic vision', different options must be considered. A Business Plan considers all the options and selects the most appropriate, to meet the ultimate objective of the business. If we could all see the results of the Plan before embarking upon it, many more Plans would be correct. In the final analysis, success of the Plan will be judged once the results are known. If the end objectives are met, the Plan will probably be judged as successful. Since few claim to have clairvoyant powers, techniques have evolved to help evaluate whether the Plan is right by projecting what is likely to happen if the Plan is adopted. For any Business Plan, the minimum step that is undertaken is to judge whether the Plan will be successful before its implementation, by projecting what is likely to happen – just to ensure the Plan does meet its objectives, at least at the outset.

Put more simply, you can come up with the most brilliant ideas in the world but the question still remains, 'Will they work?' There are two crushing problems. If you solve them both, you are in business. One of the problems we looked at in the last section: Can you convince a banker or investor that you have a successful Business Plan? The other is: Do you have the right Plan in the first place – do you end up achieving your main objective? Growth can never be a long-term objective in itself. In the business world the ultimate goal is to make profits.

Some Basics for Preparing the Plan

You have come up with some brilliant ideas for the business, and you know how to present them convincingly. The ideas may be to consolidate the business or to develop it into new activities. Now is the time to find out if the ideas are sound. The Plan must now be realistically costed.

The essence of business has not changed for centuries. It is only the techniques that have changed. The key to success is earning more from sales than the cost incurred in making those sales. Only costs which relate to those sales are counted. Costs of goods which are for future sales, for example, are excluded from costs. So are costs of buying fixed assets, even though the organization has paid for them. Conversely, costs incurred at other times are included if they relate to sales being made now. Depreciation is the allocation of past costs of buying assets to current sales, for example.

The Plan is made up of two components. The first is Profits – an objective in itself. The other establishes whether the framework exists which allows the company to trade at the proposed level of activity. It is the amount of cash outflow needed now, but which relates to future periods – the amount of investment needed to achieve those profits. One cannot be achieved without the other. No Plan is finished without having dealt with both.

But before you start, there are three things you should bear in mind. Ignore them at your peril!

Realism

Many a Plan has failed because of undue optimism. Be realistic about costs and margins. The first step of the Plan, forecasting future results, uses historic information. Make sure it is accurate. If there is any doubt, get it audited, internally or externally, but make sure it is correct. It is the best guide to how you have been doing. Because time is needed to extract up-to-date, accurate information, this stage should not be rushed.

Involvement by the right people

There is an important principle in forecasting overheads and margins which reflect the planned activities of the business. Accountants who are not fully involved in cost control and devising the Plan of activities of the company cannot possibly be expected to project realistically. They will not know how margins will be affected by the Plan. They will also stab in the dark as to which costs will be saved and which resources must be extended to achieve the Plan. Costs arising from additional resources may include: increasing the number of staff, the amount of travel, the level of additional typing, the complexity of debt collection. These costs can only be known by the person entrusted to implement that part of the Plan.

Similarly, the people who have inspired and built the Plan are unlikely to have been fully involved in preparation of the historic accounts. They cannot sensibly be expected to grasp the nuances of the historical information in order to be able to project effectively past costs to the future. They may miss abnormal patterns in historical information which will not be repeated in the future. This applies as much to abnormally low costs as to exceptionally high ones. They may easily fail to properly associate business resources, such as staff and finance, with the true and full costs reflected in the historic accounts.

The moral is to treat the planning process with the respect it deserves and ensure everyone is fully involved in all aspects of the Plan. It means accountants should be fully involved in meetings and discussions which create the growth Plan. It also means the Plan's architects should participate fully in considering and projecting details of expected costs and margins, in conjunction with the Finance people.

Finance

The final warning relates to Finance. Finance is to business what brake fluid is to brakes. It doesn't matter how good the design of a brake system is if there isn't enough brake fluid in the system. If there is a leak and the system is unable to cope with leaks, the design will also fail. If a business has not arranged adequate funding or has not allowed for extra funds in the event that things do not go fully to Plan, and extra funds turn out to be needed, no matter how well the business has been planned, it will fail. The same care must be taken, therefore, in planning funding as in devising the Plan for profits in the first place.

Chapter Summary

- The Planning process must consider various methods of achieving the Company Objectives, and select the best.
- When carrying out this evaluation, there are three important rules to follow. Forecasts must be realistic. The right people should be involved in the process. And the level of funding needed to achieve the objectives must be considered. The funding aspect is almost as important to the evaluation as deciding which of the options is most profitable.

9 The Sales and Margins Plan

Planning the future of your business demands consideration of the following: analysis of areas of activity; sales forecast; cost of sales forecast; using the margins Plan; developing the margins Plan.

The ground rules for devising the Business Plan are described in the previous chapter. This chapter covers the normal first step to costing a Plan once the strategy has been devised.

You propose a strategy. If the proposal turns out to be too risky or if it fails to achieve the objective, you will not move in that direction. To find out whether you believe it will work, you project what you think will happen if you implement the strategy, falling back on your experience to judge uncertainties. Most businesses start to cost the Plan with a Sales forecast. The Plan is worked through in theory over the next year or so.

After this, the reaction of the customers is considered. For example, what happens if they buy less? What happens if suppliers are unable to supply in full? The effect of each possibility is quantified. Then, when all such important possibilities have been considered and evaluated, the move is made – the Plan is fixed. This chapter deals with some of the considerations for 'working through' the Plan. The first step is to project what you expect is most likely to happen.

In the final analysis, companies Plan for profits. If they choose to expand, it is for the extra profits that come from expansion. Many companies confuse growth of sales with growth of profits. Whereas one may well result in the other, that is not always the case. It makes sense to put more emphasis on creating a Plan which is aimed at maximizing profit, that is, the gross profit margin, rather than the more restricted aim to maximize how many sales in total are made. Since the margins Plan is a logical extension to the sales Plan, the emphasis of this review deals with maximizing margins.

Analysis of Areas of Activities

Before the Margins Plan can commence, divide the company's activities into its product ranges. Keep subdividing the activities until each product is divided into the parts whose characteristics are similar. The reason for this apparently simple exercise is to make it easier to forecast margins, and the costs of achieving those margins. For reasons illustrated more fully below, this division can have a dramatic effect on the success of the Plan. A few words on this subdivision may be helpful.

Grouping activities with similar characteristics means identifying those activities with similar patterns of gross profits on each sale, those activities which are marketed in similar ways – and therefore, have similar costs of selling – those whose customers come from the same markets, and those whose costs of production are similar and whose acquisition costs are alike.

There is a marble company, for example, which buys marble and manipulates it. They lay it on floors and walls in buildings. They also make furniture with it. Their analysis groups tables sold to households separately from tables sold to offices. This is because they are marketed differently, despite them having the same costs of production. By contrast, marble used to make office furniture is distinguished from marble used on office walls because the supply process, administration and funding requirements of the two activities are so different. This grouping is chosen even though the same customer and material is involved.

This analysis provides a foundation for forecasting. It is also useful for controlling the business in the future by separating activities which need different types of management and funding.

Sales Forecast

Now comes the crunch of any Business Plan – predicting sales. Predict the volume of sales by quantity, weight, time or other measures by which you price your sales. Forecast sales value only after this step is complete. This type of projection is more understandable. It allows easier evaluation of the effects of changing the company's sales prices. It makes it easier to see the effects of deviating from the Plan later on in the process.

If you are not careful, this division can become too detailed to be of use. As a rough guide, if grouping results in less than 10% of the total sales and margin, its distinction is probably too excessive.

The next step is easy. Set out the average price for each unit, for each area of activity. The resulting table now gives the value of the sales, the sales forecast (see Table 9.1).

This combination of volume sales and unit prices in one table provides a useful tool for a number of reasons:

Table 9.1 **Sales forecast model**

FORECAST OF TURNOVER
FOR THE YEAR ENDING
31 DECEMBER 1993

£'000

	Commercial	Private	Total
Marble			
Construction	7,797	1,008	8,805
Furniture	427	1,075	1,502
Labour			
Installation	5,100	2,194	7,294
Design	1,314	469	1,783
	14,638	4,746	19,384

BY VOLUME

	Commercial	Private	Total
MARBLE – CONSTRUCTION			
Floor area			
(sq.m. '000)	1,000	110	1,110
Average sales price	7.80	9.16	7.93
Average mark up			
on cost	1.15	1.55	1.19
Sales Value	7,797	1,008	8,805
MARBLE – FURNITURE			
Tables (number '000)	4.5	6.0	10.5
Average sales price	94.81	179.10	142.98
Average mark up			
on cost	2.50	3.80	3.31
Sales Value	426.6	1,074.6	1,501.2
LABOUR – INSTALLATION			
Sq. Meters installed			
('000)	400	90	490
Labour per sq.m.	8.50	9.75	8.73
Mark up	1.5	2.5	1.71
Sales Value	5,100	2,194	7,294
LABOUR – DESIGN			
Hours sold ('000)	27.0	5.0	32.0
Cost per hour	32.44	37.50	33.23
Mark up per hour	1.5	2.5	1.68
Sales Value	1,313.8	468.8	1,782.6

- It eases evaluating the effect on margins of changing selling prices. It forces you to differentiate between increase or decrease of prices from decreases or increases of sales volumes.
- It encourages you to look at whether stock holdings are plausable. Stock, in volume terms, is the difference between purchase volumes and sales volumes. Often, apparently realistic projected stock holdings are clearly impossible when looked at in terms of the volume of stocks. Looking at projected stock volumes is useful as a basis for controlling stock levels in future.
- It often provides a simple table for calculating the cost of sales.

Costs of Sales Forecast

The next tier to the Margins Plan is analysing the cost of sales. Heated debates have raged for years about which costs should be included within cost of sales. The theoreticians argue that any cost should be included which arises from generating sales. They add to the purchase costs, costs of distribution, salaries of the sales team, advertising costs, even a proportion of overheads that relate to the sales effort. The purists rant about a direct linkage of a cost to a particular sale. Any cost which is the direct result of a sale, such as materials and sales commissions would be included. But general advertising and other non-specific costs are strictly relegated to overheads.

Which of the two is right? In truth, if either were more correct than the other, the argument would not continue. Either is correct, whichever you feel more comfortable with. In the model Plans at the end of this book, only the direct costs were included within the cost of sales since it was easier to experiment with the effect on margins of alternate sales methods and pricing structures.

Ideally, costs of sales should be separated into the same sort of categories as sales. Where this can be done, the Margins Plan looks like Table 9.3.

Margins Forecast

The gross profit forecast is simply the combination of the sales and cost of sales forecasts. This is illustrated in Table 9.2.

Table 9.2 **Margins Plan**

£'000

	Commercial	(%)	Private	(%)	Total	(%)
Marble						
Construction	1,017	13%	358	36%	1,375	16%
Furniture	256	60%	792	74%	1,048	70%
Labour						
Installation	1,700	33%	1,316	60%	3,016	41%
Design	438	33%	281	60%	719	40%
	3,411	23%	2,747	58%	6,159	32%

Table 9.3 **Margins forecast model**

FORECAST OF COST OF SALES
FOR THE YEAR ENDING
31 DECEMBER 1993

£'000

	Commercial	Private	Total
Marble			
Construction	6,780	650	7,430
Furniture	171	283	454
Labour			
Installation	3,400	878	4,278
Design	876	188	1,064
	11,227	1,999	13,226

BY VOLUME

	Commercial	Private	Total
MARBLE – CONSTRUCTION			
Floor area			
('000 sq.m.)	1,000	110	1,110
Ave cost (£/sq.m.)	6.78	5.91	6.69
Cost Value	6,780	650	7,430
MARBLE – FURNITURE			
Tables (number '000)	4.5	6.0	10.5
Ave marble per unit			
(sq.m.)	0.80	0.75	0.77
Average marble cost			
(£/sq.m.)	6.78	5.91	6.28
Average labour cost			
per unit	32.50	42.70	38.33
Cost Value	170.6	282.8	453.3
LABOUR			
Labour per sq.m.	8.50	9.75	8.73
Sq. Meters installed			
('000)	400	90	490
Cost Value	3,400	878	4,278
DESIGN			
Hours sold ('000)	27.0	5.0	32.0
Cost per hour	32.44	37.50	33.23
Cost Value	875.9	187.5	1,063.4

Using the Margins Plan

Many companies have costs which do not link so easily with sales. For these companies, there is usually an element of costs which vary directly with sales. There are also other costs which are fixed, regardless of how much is sold. It is difficult to allocate costs which do not vary to sales. But there is a simple solution; do not try to. It is better to predict variable costs accurately, and separately control and project fixed costs, rather than merging the two and reducing the level of accuracy and usability of the results. The difficulty of not allocating all costs of sales is in interpretation. Which area of activity is inefficient, for example, if two activities each produce reasonable margins but are inadequate to cover fixed costs of production? The answer is not simple. The conventional solution of dividing fixed costs between activities is arbitrary and provides what appears to be a simple solution. But the simplicity is likely to cause inaccurate decisions to be made. A simple example to contrast the methods is set out in Table 9.4.

In the evaluation, it may be tempting to eliminate the retail activities on the basis that the division does not make sufficient margins, whereas the fuller review is more likely to lead to the conclusion that the whole Shoes activity is unprofitable. Solving the problem is more likely to be correct without the arbitrary allocation of fixed costs. But the fuller evaluation must not forget to take full account of the fixed costs in evaluation. Again, it is not necessary to become too involved in trying to get accurate divisions or allocations. It is often impossible. Just get reasonably close.

It cannot be stressed enough how important the division of activities is to the Plan. If the categories are appropriate, forecasting and evaluation are likely to be useful. If the categories are inappropriate, forecasts are likely to be less realistic and, from a control angle, potentially misleading. In view of its importance, if there is any doubt about the categorization, professional advice may be particularly beneficial.

Developing the Margins Plan

Once the margins have been forecast, you might be tempted to move on to overheads. But you would be missing one of the most important single aspects of the Plan – experimentation.

Some people call it 'What if! analysis', some call it 'Sensitivity analysis'. Others think of it as 'Contingency planning'. Whatever its name, it is useful to see what is the effect on Margins of varying different components of the Plan. This can help understand how much can be gained or lost from being either over- or under-optimistic. It is also useful for planning how the business should best operate in future. Which products should be expanded, what pricing is optimum, how should the company react to underperformance of specific segments of its business? (See Chapters 13 and 14.) There is still value, even at this stage, to go through some initial experiments.

For each activity, plot the effect on margins (sales and cost of sales) of different sales volumes. Plot the effect of both increases and decreases. The range of variations should cover:

Table 9.4
Costs not allocated according to turnover

£'000

	Bags	‹ -------- Shoes -------- ›		Fixed cost	Total
		Wholesale	Retail		
Sales	2,000	1,500	2,000		5,500
Cost of sales					
Bought in	1,500			500	2,000
Materials		400	600		1,000
Labour		200	600	400	1,200
Machinery				1,000	1,000
Total costs	1,500	600	1,200	1,900	5,200
Gross Profits	500	900	800	−1,900	300

Costs allocated according to turnover

	Bags	‹ -------- Shoes -------- ›		Fixed cost	Total
		Wholesale	Retail		
Sales	2,000	1,500	2,000		5,500
Cost of sales					
Bought in	1,500			500	2,000
Materials		400	600		1,000
Labour		200	600	400	1,200
Machinery				1,000	1,000
Reallocation of costs		814	1,086	−1,900	0
Total costs	1,500	1,414	2,286	0	5,200
Gross Profits	500	86	−286	0	300

- The worst possible plausible scenario
- A drop of turnover of, say, 15%, 10% and 5% of volume
- An increase of turnover of the same amount
- The best possible plausible scenario

These should all be considered without changing the 'spend' on marketing.

The reworking of forecasts with different sales levels is not designed to give exercise to your personal computer. Rather, it is only of value if you consider carefully how you, your customers and competitors would react to the change. If relevant, the gross margin or fixed costs should be changed. If, for example, reducing turnover by 10% meant salaries would be reduced, reduce them in the forecast. It is the realism you inject into the Sensitivity analysis that makes it worthwhile.

Then go through each product plotting the effect of changing prices, of both purchases and sales separately. Increasing the price will decrease the volume. But the net effect on total turnover is not always as expected. The value of this analysis is the evaluation of the benefit or costs of stimulating different aspects of the business, either by expansion, contraction or simply increasing efficiency. If you bargain your suppliers down to the threshold of goodwill, how much is saved, and what is the contrary effect on reliability and service they provide? If you give pay increases, how much of the rise should be passed on to customers? If a discount structure is proposed, are profits enhanced, and by how much, or will you simply be giving away a part of your profits to customers?

Table 9.5 **Sensitivity model**

SALES AND MARGINS SENSITIVITY ANALYSIS
FOR THE YEAR ENDING
31 DECEMBER 1992

£'000	Sales	Gross Profits	Overheads	Net Profits
Best possible scenario @ 15% above target	14,375	4,888	3,950	938
7.5% above target	13,438	4,569	3,800	769
Target	12,500	4,250	3,600	650
5% below target	11,875	4,038	3,600	438
10% below target	11,250	3,800	3,400	400
20% below target	10,000	3,100	3,200	−100
Worst possible scenario @ 25% below target	9,375	2,950	3,200	−250

Note: In the above example, the company assumed that it would have to reduce its margins if turnover dropped below 10% lower than target. The directors had identified a number of contingency plans to reduce overheads if turnover looked as if it may fall by more than 5% below target.

Once turnover looked as if it may fall below 20%, the company was due to make losses. The Directors were now at the stage of considering the risk of this occurring. If they believed the risk to be sufficiently low, they would not take any drastic action at this stage. However, if the perceived risk was not negligible, they would have to think harder about how overheads could be reduced even more or margins increased to compensate. Alternatively, the Directors may have to reconsider whether the plan they initially set out may need to be modified.

The Directors noted that the reason why the company would potentially go into a loss position was that overheads had been increased significantly in order to achieve a desired development route. This increase in risk would have to be considered in relation to the projected benefits before deciding whether to adopt the Plan.

These analyses are not put in the report. But their production is crucial to an awareness of how realistic the Business Plan is. It is also needed to understand how sensitive it is to deviate from target and what the effect is of modifying the Plan.

Before moving on, there are two potential problems you may have to deal with. First, you may not have the detailed historical information to be able to analyse the forecasts in the necessary detail. Make sure the problem is resolved for next year's planning. For this year, estimates are the next best thing. But for each figure estimated, add in extra margins for error when doing the sensitivity analyses. The more difficult you find it to make meaningful estimates, the less risk should be taken. Even if no real value can be gained from analysis, the attempt is still worthwhile. It provides a benchmark to compare future results and provides valuable experience for future forecasts.

The second problem is that historic information may be available, but it may be inaccurate. It is always worth summarizing forecasts and comparing them with audited accounts. It may throw out some surprises before a banker or investor does it for you. It is also worth, in some cases, arranging for the historic information itself to be audited. There is little more frustrating than a Business Plan that has failed because it was based on fantasy figures. It is the one thing bankers and investors never seem to forgive.

Do not mislead yourself into believing that producing the product information on a regular basis is a luxury or impractical in view of the time needed to get the information. The only resources needed are discipline and correct accounting procedures. The extra information then takes no further time to produce.

Chapter Summary

- The first step to forecasting profits is to divide the company's trade into its most appropriate activities. The division should not be too detailed, but it should be sufficiently detailed to allow it to be used for planning later on.
- The next step is to forecast sales. Both the value and the volume of sales must be predicted for each activity.
- The direct costs involved in achieving those sales is then projected.
- The end result of the sales and cost of sales forecasts is the margins forecast. The information is used to evaluate the most profitable mix of activities.
- The figures should be experimented with. You should consider the effect on volume and margins of changing prices and changing the marketing strategy. This should leave you with a good understanding of the optimum marketing position the business should adopt, in terms of both pricing relative to competitors and the level of marketing effort.

10   The Overheads Plan

'A business that doesn't know what its costs are will succeed about as easily as a learner driver who doesn't know where the brakes are.'

Traditionally, overheads are easier to forecast than any other part of the Plan. They tend to contain the more controllable costs of the business. But often, planning and control of overheads is carried out at a detailed level with little thought given to the overview. Business planning requires more of a 'wood control' policy than a 'tree chopping' exercise.

Analysis of Costs

There are many ways to analyse overheads – the level of detail desired and the nature of cost usually provide a logical division. Getting the most appropriate division is so important for planning that there may be benefit from getting professional assistance in the absence of obvious analysis. A form of analysis which is appropriate to many businesses is:

- Establishment costs
- Personnel costs
- Personnel running costs
- Legal and professional
- Finance costs
- Selling and marketing
- Equipment costs
- Research and development
- Other

Establishment costs

These are the direct costs of accommodating the business. They include the direct costs of rent, rates and service charges. They also include related costs of repairs and maintenance to premises and insurance of premises. These are, as far as possible, the costs that would disappear if the business moved out of the premises.

Personnel costs

These are the direct costs of staff, including national insurance, pensions and any other employment incentives or benefits provided to staff.

Personnel running costs

These are the costs of running the business from the premises. In theory, they disappear if personnel stop work. They tend to vary in proportion to the number of people employed. They include the cost of the telephone, light and heat, general insurances, costs of running motor vehicles, cleaning, teas, coffee etc.

Finance costs

These are the costs of funding business assets which are not covered by equity or retained profits and which have been paid for. Their costs have no direct correlation with the level of sales of the business and need specific control. It includes overdraft and loan interest and interest costs of hire purchase and leasing arrangement.

Selling/marketing

These are the costs of marketing. They include direct costs such as advertising, salaries of the sales team, the cost of exhibitions and promotions. This category sets out the Company's resources allocated to achieving sales.

Equipment costs

This category evaluates the cost of equipment. It includes the cost of depreciating equipment, the cost of repairs and maintenance of equipment. It provides guidance about the cost of improving or reducing the level of equipment used by a business.

Research and Development

This is the cost of Research and Development of a business. It includes relevant salaries
and equipment and other costs which would disappear if the Research and Development
programme of the business were to be stopped.

  Once costs have been appropriately categorized, they should be forecast. The level
of overheads must reflect the level of activities forecast in the margins Plan. It is useful
to predict the number of people needed to sustain the level of business forecast, since
so much of the cost of overheads spins off from the number of people employed. For
example:

Table 10.1 **Personnel Totals**

(Cost in '000)	Jan – Jul	Aug – Nov	Dec
Sales Dept			
Personnel	7	9	12
Admin.	4	6	8
Cost/month	220	300	400
Administration			
Personnel	6	6	6
Cost/month	96	96	116
Production			
Personnel	14	18	22
Cost/month	182	234	312
Totals			
Personnel	31	39	48
Cost/month	498	630	828

The overall profit forecasts can now be brought together. A typical example is set out
in Table 10.2. Chapters 20 and 21 have other examples of fully detailed profit and loss
accounts in their Appendices.

Establishment Costs

Establishment costs should be easy to forecast. The size and location of selected premises should be listed and the related cost charted. Where part of the floor area is used
for manufacturing or for other overhead categories, the direct establishment cost should
be apportioned on the basis of floor area, if this is appropriate. Where there is any
doubt about where to leave the cost, it is usually better to leave the part that is in
doubt in Establishment costs. The effect of varying both the size and location of premises
should be considered to determine whether advantages can be gained from fundamental
changes.

Table 10.2　Full profit forecast

PROJECTED PROFIT & LOSS ACCOUNT
FOR THE YEAR ENDED
31 DECEMBER 1992

£'000

	Jan. 1992	Feb.	March	April	May	June	July	August	Sept.	Oct.	Nov.	Dec.	Total
SALES	1,120	1,210	1,300	1,430	1,350	1,100	890	920	1,100	1,460	1,290	1,100	14,270
COST OF SALES Purchases	784	847	910	1,001	945	770	623	644	770	1,022	903	770	9,989
GROSS PROFIT	336	363	390	429	405	330	267	276	330	438	387	330	4,281
GROSS PROFIT	30%	30%	30%	30%	30%	30%	30%	30%	30%	30%	30%	30%	30%
OVERHEADS Cash payments (See Table 10.3)	207	227	222	218	223	220	220	230	230	228	231	222	2,678
Depreciation	41	42	42	42	42	43	43	43	43	43	43	43	510
	248	268	264	260	266	263	263	273	273	271	274	265	3,188
OPERATING PROFIT	88	95	126	169	139	67	4	3	57	167	113	65	1,093
TAXATION													0
NET PROFIT	88	95	126	169	139	67	4	.3	57	167	113	65	1,093

Personnel Costs

Personnel costs should be easy to predict once the number and level of staff has been identified. The risk of misevaluating the number of personnel needed to effect the volume of sales and production is often one of the most serious causes of failure to meet targets. The risk is particularly high where the management have little experience of running a business at the forecast levels of activities.

Start with the historic staffing levels and assume the number of people needed will increase in proportion to increased volumes. If there are any factors which may increase or decrease the cost, such as a Plan to improve the quality of staff, to make use of economies of scale, to change work practices or introduce incentives, these should be clearly identified to justify deviation from the basic assumption.

Personnel running costs tend to change in proportion to the number of staff employed. Again, there may be planned reasons why variations occur, but they should be identified and reasoned before deviating from the expected. As an overview, each cost should be reviewed separately considering radical change. The effect on margins and productivity should be considered to evaluate how effectively that overhead resource is being applied.

Other Costs

The costs of marketing, equipment, and research and development are all key to running the business. Each should be considered with regard to radical change to establish the effect on margins and net profits. This type of evaluation is more successful with the more creativity that you can apply. Brainstorming sessions, business books, consultants and personnel ideas are all possible sources of inspiration which may improve the effectiveness of expenditure on resources. It may also allow a decrease in the level of costs to occur at no loss to the organization.

Finance Costs

An arithmetic calculation determines the costs of finance. It should be recalculated each time a new Plan is considered. There are a number of controllable factors which affect this cost. These include the level of expenditure on assets, the speed of payment to suppliers, the resources devoted to debt collection and discount policies. There is also a degree of control over the rate of interest by fixing interest rates over a period, restructuring overall borrowings – including hire purchase and other similar arrangements – and by increasing the level of equity or retained profits.

In any event, the level of borrowings rarely moves in the direction expected and has little correlation with the level of sales. It is important, therefore, to re-calculate this cost at the end of the forecasting process, once other decisions have been made.

OVERHEADS WITH A CASH FLOW EFFECT
FOR THE YEAR ENDED
31 DECEMBER 1992
£'000

	Jan. 1992	Feb.	March	April	May	June	July	August	Sept.	Oct.	Nov.	Dec.	Total
ESTABLISHMENT													
Rent	10.0	10.0	10.0	10.0	10.0	10.0	10.0	10.0	10.0	10.0	10.0	10.0	120.0
Rates	3.0	3.0	3.0	3.0	3.0	3.0	3.0	3.0	3.0	3.0	3.0	3.0	36.0
PERSONNEL RUNNING COSTS													
Telephone	4.0	4.0	4.0	4.0	4.0	4.0	4.0	4.0	4.0	4.0	4.0	4.0	48.0
Prin.post.stat.	3.0	3.0	3.0	3.0	3.0	3.0	3.0	3.0	3.0	3.0	3.0	3.0	36.0
Light & heat	1.0	1.0	1.0	1.0	1.0	1.0	1.0	1.0	1.0	1.0	1.0	1.0	12.0
Insurance	3.0	3.0	3.0	3.0	3.0	3.0	3.0	3.0	3.0	3.0	3.0	3.0	36.0
Cleaning	0.4	0.4	0.4	0.4	0.4	0.4	0.4	0.4	0.4	0.4	0.4	0.4	4.8
Motor expenses	5.0	5.0	5.0	5.0	5.0	5.0	5.0	5.0	5.0	5.0	5.0	5.0	60.0
Travel	8.0	8.0	8.0	8.0	8.0	8.0	8.0	8.0	8.0	8.0	8.0	8.0	96.0
Entertaining	4.0	4.0	4.0	4.0	4.0	4.0	4.0	4.0	4.0	4.0	4.0	4.0	48.0
Repairs	6.0	6.0	6.0	6.0	6.0	6.0	6.0	6.0	6.0	6.0	6.0	6.0	72.0
Sundry expenses	5.0	5.0	5.0	5.0	5.0	5.0	5.0	5.0	5.0	5.0	5.0	5.0	60.0
PERSONNEL COSTS													
Directors remuneration	10.0	10.0	10.0	10.0	10.0	10.0	10.0	10.0	10.0	10.0	10.0	10.0	120.0
Wages & salaries	30.0	30.0	30.0	30.0	30.0	30.0	30.0	30.0	30.0	30.0	30.0	30.0	360.0
National insurance	41.0	41.0	41.0	41.0	41.0	41.0	41.0	41.0	41.0	41.0	41.0	41.0	492.0
ADMINISTRATIVE COSTS													
Legal & professional	3.0	3.0	3.0	3.0	3.0	3.0	3.0	3.0	3.0	3.0	3.0	3.0	36.0
Audit & accountancy	5.0	5.0	5.0	5.0	5.0	5.0	5.0	5.0	5.0	5.0	5.0	5.0	60.0
EQUIPMENT COSTS													
Hire of equipment	4.0	4.0	4.0	4.0	4.0	4.0	4.0	4.0	4.0	4.0	4.0	4.0	48.0
													0.0
	145.4	145.4	145.4	145.4	145.4	145.4	145.4	145.4	145.4	145.4	145.4	145.4	1,744.8
SELLING & DISTRIBUTION													
Advertising	20.0	20.0	20.0	20.0	20.0	20.0	20.0	20.0	20.0	20.0	20.0	20.0	240.0
Carriage	5.0	5.0	5.0	5.0	5.0	5.0	5.0	5.0	5.0	5.0	5.0	5.0	60.0
Sales commission	10.0	10.0	10.0	10.0	10.0	10.0	10.0	10.0	10.0	10.0	10.0	10.0	120.0
Marketing	15.0	15.0	15.0	15.0	15.0	15.0	15.0	15.0	15.0	15.0	15.0	15.0	180.0
	50.0	50.0	50.0	50.0	50.0	50.0	50.0	50.0	50.0	50.0	50.0	50.0	600.0
FINANCIAL													0.0
Bank charges	0.5	0.5	0.5	0.5	0.5	0.5	0.5	0.5	0.5	0.5	0.5	0.5	6.0
Bank interest 15%	11.2	30.8	25.7	22.1	27.4	24.0	24.3	33.7	34.2	32.2	35.1	25.9	326.6
	11.7	31.3	26.2	22.6	27.9	24.5	24.8	34.2	34.7	32.7	35.6	26.4	332.6
TOTAL	207.1	226.7	221.6	218.0	223.3	219.9	220.2	229.6	230.1	228.1	231.0	221.8	2,677.4

Sundry Points

Historic information

As with all other planning forecasting, any projections based on historic information can never be better than the information on which they are based. An error becomes tragic if resources are committed to the wrong area for want of accurate information which would indicate the error before the outset.

Extent of analysis

As with the Margins Plan, the degree of analysis and accuracy of the Overheads Plan is necessary only as far as the outcome would be significantly affected by the review.

Sensitivity analysis

The overheads should be 'valued', even before performing the full Risk Analysis described in Chapters 13 and 14. Each overhead should be considered in turn. The cost should be compared to the margins achieved. The purpose is to see how 'efficient' the cost is. This can be a particularly useful review for adding realism to the most likely overhead structure.

To carry out the review, each cost is considered by reference to how much margin might be lost if the cost was reduced. This process emphasizes on which overheads the business is dependent, and which overheads are too low or too high in the forecast. Professional advice may help improve the quality of the review.

If it becomes apparent during the review that some of the projected overheads were wrong, they should be changed in the final Plan.

Chapter Summary

- The first step to forecasting overheads is to divide the company's costs into useful categories.
- The overheads which must be incurred to achieve projected turnover should be predicted. If a high marketing spend is needed to achieve the forecast level of turnover, for example, that level of marketing cost must be included in the forecast.
- The forecast costs can be based on historic costs. But the historic costs must be checked to ensure they are accurate and fully understood.
- Once the forecasts are complete, analyses should be carried out to quantify the effect of possible error. Firstly the effect of the less controllable or predictable costs getting out of hand should be evaluated. Secondly, an evaluation should consider how overheads would be increased or decreased if different levels of turnover are targeted.

11 The Funding Plan

'Nothing is worse than being told for the first time a week before a business is going to run out of cash. It hardly inspires confidence to inject more cash.'

What is the biggest single cause of business failure? Is it making losses? Is it losing key management? Is it competition? Would it surprise you if running out of money were the answer?

Whenever the economic cycle is in expansive bloom, there is a surplus of funds available for business. Since deregulation of the banking industry in 1988, newly released competition exaggerated the cyclical availability of funds for business, until 1990. Business got used to easy finance – or relatively easy finance – but for exactly this reason, too many loans became bad in the recession that welcomed in the new decade. Suddenly banks became unable to continue to lend the quantity of money previously at their disposal, for fear of compounding losses already being experienced. Planning a business's funding became a startlingly different operation.

The Importance Of The Funding Plan

In the past it was often the result of bad management and failure to achieve targets that caused a business to use up all its resources. There is far more money available for a business which has not run out of money than for one that has. This is one of the reasons that inadequate funding can be catastrophic for a business. It is not just the inability to make new investment, it is also the enormous drain on top management time spent dealing with raising further funding that can often reverse the outcome for an otherwise successful business.

Running out of money as a result of inadequate planning is rightly attributed to poor management. Planning a growing business should produce growing profits. Instinctively, most people assume that if profits grow, the bank balance grows and therefore less external funding will be needed. The reality is that profits take time to roll in. Even once profits are being made, it takes one year to accumulate one year's profits. Yet much before then, any investment needed will have to be funded. In addition, as a business grows, its working capital usually grows at the same rate. Sometimes, to achieve growth, the level of stock and debtors must rise in advance of the growth. It may be necessary, for example, to hold a wider stock range or take a greater buffer stock to grow. The business may start to deal with a lower-quality customer base which takes longer to pay for products. Either outcome would require disproportionate funding. And if the company is profitable and it has run out of funds, it is in the 'run out of funds' category of businesses.

If you are not yet convinced by the importance of planning funding, the following example clearly demonstrates the unpredictable nature of funding:

a) A company has £2m. turnover. Its borrowings are £500,000. Its assets are:

		£'000
Fixed assets		1,000
Stock	1,000	
Debtors	700	
Creditors	(700)	
		1,000
Total net assets		2,000
These are financed by:		
Borrowings		500
Retained equity		1,500
		2,000

b) The company's turnover doubles to £4 million, fixed assets double, stock doubles, debtors and creditors both double. By how much do borrowings increase?

   i) Stays the same
   ii) Doubles
   iii) Quadruples

c) The answer is . . . none of the above. The increase is fivefold:

		£'000
Fixed assets		2,000
Stock	2,000	
Debtors	1,400	
Creditors	(1,400)	
		2,000
Total net assets		4,000
These are financed by:		
Borrowings		2,500
Retained equity		1,500
		4,000

Borrowings have therefore risen from £500,000 in the first stage to £2,500,000 in the second.

Planning the needs of a business is not simply an arithmetic exercise to project cash flows. It requires Planning of how each aspect of the company's assets should respond to development Plans and how any additional assets are to be funded. The cash flow forecast will not begin to be meaningful until after these are all considered.

Fixed Assets

These usually comprise:

- The cost of premises (freehold or improvements as relevant)
- Plant and equipment
- Motor vehicles
- Computers
- Furniture

If turnover is Planned to double, start with the assumption that personnel will double. This is likely to require double the office or factory space, double the number of plant, computers and other equipment, and double the amount of other assets. Doubling the assets does not necessarily double the cost of assets. Sometimes it requires expenditure of more than double if current equipment is old or technologically creaking. From the basic assumption, then consider how much of each asset will be needed to implement the planned activities.

If the Business plans to develop by exploiting new technology, obtain quotes for acquiring the technology. Consider the space taken up and the extent to which new equipment substitutes for personnel and other equipment. The end result may be an increased requirement of space of, say, 40%. Some or all of that space may be accommodated by cramming in resources to existing premises, or alternative premises may be found. Whatever the final result, justify positively how space requirements vary from doubling. Then find out the cost of new space. If there is a need to move, use known figures wherever possible. Where this is not possible, look for premises to gauge a realistic level of likely costs. Where the cost of premises will be significant to the business, try out the effect of spending different amounts to see how sensitive profits and the borrowing needs are. It may help you decide where to set up shop.

The same evaluation criteria apply to each asset. Many Plans fail because of the inadequate priority planners put on this aspect of their Plan; it seems on the face of it too easy to warrant any effort. But it isn't.

Working Capital

Working capital is the value of money paid out to fund the purchase of goods, services and overheads to the extent that it precedes money received from customers for your sales. The surplus refunded by customers, the profit, is available to fund the next transaction, in part, unless it is needed to fund the purchase of fixed assets. As the level of business grows, it is not surprising that the level of purchases and overheads increases before the amount of cash inflow. It is no accident, therefore, that as a business grows, the working capital requirements increase.

The components of working capital start when the business buys goods and pays for overheads. The cost ends up as stock and creditors. Next, the creditors are paid, which creates a bank overdraft. Then stock is sold, with the creation of a debtor albeit at a higher value than the cost. During this time, overheads are paid, which increases the overdraft even further. Finally, debtors pay – all being well – creating a bank surplus. The surplus, of course, is reversed if the next round of creditors are paid before the debtors have paid in full. The total time between initially receiving goods from suppliers and finally receiving funds from debtors is called the 'working capital cycle'. Its illustration in numbers is:

Stock	1,000
Trade debtors	500
Bank overdraft	(500)
Trade creditors	(700)
Total working capital	300

As may be evident, if a company's working capital cycle increases, so does the level of funding needed. If the business development affects the length of the working capital cycle, its effect must not be overlooked. To forecast the extent to which the working capital will change if the Plan is implemented, each component needs to be considered separately.

The technique may be becoming familiar. Assume each component will stay the same size relative to turnover and purchases. Assume debtors will become a constant percentage of turnover, and stock and creditors have a fixed ratio to purchases. The level of working capital becomes simple for forecast. However, there may be Plans to control the level of working capital. There may be scope for reducing the company's funding requirements and costs if the level of working capital can be reduced. In contrast, there may be little scope for avoiding an increase in the level of funding needs if the company grows or if the pattern of trading changes. Either way, there is good reason to control working capital.

From this basic challenge each assumption individually, with regard to the planned development of the business.

Stock

Controlling stock involves weighing up conflicting effects. There are cost savings from holding lower stock levels. There are potential losses from failing to make a sale, if holding inadequate levels of stock means you are not able to supply specific orders from customers in time. With many organizations, stock comprises a base level of stock, which includes a minimum level of materials or stock lines, such as tools or samples. This base level of stock varies in unexpected ways compared with the desired level of overall stock holdings. In some organizations, this base stock does not vary with the level of activities, in others it varies by exactly the same as turnover. For some, the base level of stock must increase disproportionately to allow changes in trading patterns. The nature of base stock should be clearly identified to establish the first part of the forecast stock levels.

The next part of stock is routine stocks. The Plan may be to reduce or increase the number of stock lines. It may demand suppliers to hold more stocks or to supply less, but more frequently. Stock control can be a vital part of the funding needs of a company and needs to be carefully considered. The forecast level of stocks must reflect the Plan. And it must also ensure Plans to reduce stocks are achievable. It is a fool's saving to pretend that stocks can be reduced by more than they can, since the extra stock holdings will have to be funded. If the funding arranged is inadequate to finance the actual level of stocks, this may be a devastating mistake.

Debtors

The planned debtors are controllable to the extent that resources are diverted towards debt collection. This might involve allocating people to collect debts, or implementation of discount policies to encourage early payment by debtors. Whatever the Plan designates, this must be reflected in the forecasting. The basic assumption that the debtors patterns of payment will remain constant is a good start point. However, it is important to consider whether there is sufficient control to enforce this, or whether there have been any unusual factors which have affected the past performance, which will reverse. If there are any new areas of business, care should be taken not to underestimate how long it takes to collect debts in circumstances. This is a particular risk area when the type of customer to be dealt with in future is different from the type previously dealt with.

Evaluate debtors and creditors in terms of the length of time taken to pay, as in the example below:

Debtors		1,800,000
Sales	Month	Cumulative
Current month	1,200,000	1,200,000
Previous month	700,000	1,900,000
Previous month	800,000	2,700,000

Debts are a little under two months on average.

When considering whether there are any circumstances which will cause the length of debts to change, remember that recessions cause a lengthening of the debt collection period, whereas booms do the opposite. Improved debt collection usually reduces the level of debts, but at the cost of increasing overheads. A common problem of developing business is the lengthening of the debt collection period. It reflects the need to improve control as a company develops. It is possible to avoid this, but it is wise to allow a few days extra collection as a contingency.

Creditors

Whilst some buyers can pass on lengthening debt collection period to their suppliers, others may not have this pressure value. It is worth negotiating extended credit payment terms with suppliers. This helps to gauge how likely the business is to achieve this result. Forecasting the credit period may then be eased.

There are various other creditors, such as Corporation Tax, VAT and accruals whose values should be calculated. They tend to vary in proportion to the level of overheads. Where possible, liabilities should be calculated on the basis of the forecast, such as VAT and Corporation Tax.

Cash Flow Forecast

Once all the above forecasts have been made, the cash flow forecast can be prepared. Once profits, assets and liabilities have been forecast, the cash flow forecast becomes an arithmetic exercise. Once it has been prepared, it is important to look at the end results before proceeding. Sometimes, the cash flow forecasts, which pull together all other forecasts, reveal obvious errors in earlier assumptions. If the level of overdraft does not follow usual patterns each line of the forecast should be considered before accepting it.

Converting a forecast of asset and liability projections to a conventional cash flow forecast is rarely carried out – which is why many cash flow forecasts contain glaring errors which are not spotted, with obvious consequences. Professional assistance may simplify the 'translation' process.

Once all forecasts have been committed to paper, the final part of preparing the first round of the Plan is arranging the funding. This is reviewed in Chapter 12.

Before leaving this section, it is useful to consider two further points.

Errors in assumptions

Errors in assumptions about assets and working capital can have a dramatic effect on funding. It is valuable to calculate alternate funding needs on the basis of alternate assumptions. Only after the preliminary forecast is complete, chart these results and consider the likelihood of these outcomes. There may be a revision in the level of funding sought.

Cost of funding

All forms of funding have some sort of cost. If the cost is interest, the additional cost must be reflected in the profits forecast. The alternate cost is reducing the equity owned by existing shareholders. The effect of a reduced share of profits should be evaluated in relation to the extra profits, to consider how worthwhile it is issuing new equity as proposed.

Chapter Summary

- The level of funding needed to achieve the profits forecast needs to be predicted.
- This involves forecasting the level of both the fixed assets needed to run the business, and the amount of working capital needed to sustain adequate stock levels, debtors and creditors.
- The cash flow forecast will be less effective, without forecasting the assets which use up and create the cash movements. As with all other forecasts, sensitivity analyses should be carried out to consider the effect of incorrect assumptions.
- The funding forecasts should be reworked for each level of activity being considered. The cost of the funding should be incorporated within the cost forecasts.

12 The Right Type of Funding

'These loan products have been around for a long time. People are only now becoming aware of them – It is not surprising therefore that they have not been used. But a lot of companies could have saved a lot of money over the last three years if they had.'

The array of types of funding that is available is quite awesome. There are many sophisticated 'investment' products being used at the moment. These include 'ratchet' investing, 'redeemable' and 'convertible' instruments and 'option' arrangements. Each variety of source has its own variety of sub-products. Each sub-variety seems to have its own choices. Types of funding range from types suitable for everyone, to tailor-made alternatives which require an MBS qualification to understand the titles. Costs, availability, suitability, complexity – the choice seems endless.

One thing is clear. Few businesses have more than the vaguest awareness of the market – and even fewer give due weighting to selecting the type of funding they prefer.

Background

Despite the prolific number of funding products around, there are in substance only three core sources, around which all the others are based. Although they are well known, the sources are explained to highlight the relevant characteristics. The sources are as follows:

1 **Trade Credit** This comes from suppliers or tax authorities who are prepared to let you have goods or incur a tax liability before paying.

2 *Loans* These range between informal Directors' loans, bank overdrafts and formal long term loans.

3 *Equity* This is where funds are given to the business where repayment is not expected. Instead, the investor gets back the investment and makes profit from future dividends or by selling their share of the company later.

Variations on the above theme arise in a number of ways:

- The details of categories can be tailored. Loans, for example, can be short or long term and can have fixed or variable rates of interest. Equity can have differing rights and can attract fixed rate or variable dividends – some are transferable, others are not.
- A funding source can have properties from more than one category. Redeemable preference shares, for example, have some properties of equity in that they have some voting rights and attract a share of the company on winding up, but they also have properties of a loan, since they may be repaid.
- The properties may switch categories during their life. Some loans are convertible to equity after a number of years. A variety of this variation is where the properties switch conditional upon a certain event, or at the option of a third party. By creative use of these features, it is possible to arrange funds to be raised on terms that are suitable if one thing happens – such as monies being repaid if good profits are being made – but different if that thing does not happen – such as the loan becoming shares if profits do not exceed a specified amount. This section can be particularly useful where raising funds is difficult and the present shareholders, who may also be Directors of the company, are unclear about how they want the business to be funded in future.

The purpose of describing the variations is to illustrate that any funding source can be broken down into its three basic components. The choice of which you prefer may change depending on different circumstances. The different products allow the source itself to change to meet your requirements.

A useful, if poorly used, advisory facility that banks, investment companies and professional advisors provide is, 'waiting for you to ask'. Whatever the answer, ensure you understand how the answer splits into the components, and why it is being suggested as appropriate to your needs.

Investment Attributes Of Trade Credit

Attributes

Most companies are able to obtain credit from suppliers. This credit is almost always free. In a business with reasonably constant activities throughout the year, payment of one's supplier is usually replaced by credit on new transactions. There is, therefore, a core level of finance available, at no cost.

Cost

There is usually no direct cost of trade credit. This is why it is so attractive as a source of funding. Some suppliers incorporate a penalty clause for late payment. Others provide a discount for early payment. These potential costs and savings should be included within an evaluation of the cost of purchases.

Availability

Ever company should strive to negotiate as much trade credit as possible. However, where a company has cyclical or variable levels of trading, replacement credit when paying one's supplier is not always available. In practice, therefore, some of that funding may disappear at very short notice, usually at a time when the business is slowing down and alternative funding is more difficult to arrange. The same risk exists if trade credit is obtained without the full support of the supplier. Most suppliers are able to put pressure on customers to reduce the amount of trade credit they are receiving. The supplier may stop supplying or you may prefer other suppliers, with the result that payment is made more quickly.

Where there is a risk that trade credit will not be core credit, the excess should not be selected to fund the business. That is not to say that the business should not maximize the amount of trade credit, but other facilities should be arranged in advance that can be called upon if necessary. This can be by way of additional loan facilities which can be called on at a later date, or issuing share capital which is not fully paid.

Investment Attributes Of Loans

Attributes

Loans are repayable. Whether repayable in six months, ten years or on demand, they are repayable. If a business borrows a loan, it must be able to repay that loan. This is one of the key determining factors about the proportion of loan funding to equity funding that is most suitable. Loans can be repaid either by arranging replacement funding in future or by making enough profits to fund the trade, and future growth, to give income to shareholders and having sufficient to still repay the loan.

Cost

The cost of loans is interest. This reduces the profitability level of the company which, directly, reduces the value of the company.

The cost of the loan varies. It is a cost that is almost impossible to predict. Interest rates have been known to double or halve within a two-year period. The worrying feature, is that the cost of interest tends to rise at the same time that demand in the economy falls. Once the cost is incurred, it stays regardless of how well or badly the company is doing. In practice, if a company has trading difficulties, it usually needs to increase its borrowings, which in turn increases its interest cost, which compounds the problems. As costs increase in proportion to overall profits, so does the exposure of the business to failure from interest cost variations.

This is a factor that is important when considering Risk. It is worth discussing potential Risk-related problems with your bank manager. These days, there are many loan products which banks can arrange, which either wholly or partially restrict the cost of interest for chosen periods. Generally, the more risk a bank perceives a loan to be, the more expensive it will be.

Availability

Availability is another feature of loans. Generally, banks and other lenders will ensure that their loan is repaid if the business fails. The availability of loans, therefore, depends on the availability of security to protect the lender. If the company requires additional funding at some stage in the future, borrowings tend to be the fastest way to get the funds. If the company has already used up all security, it renews this route of fast funding in future. For this reason, it may be beneficial to reduce the proportion of borrowings to allow manoeuvring in future.

Choice of length of loan

Another feature of loans is their length. Overdrafts are generally repayable on demand. This means a bank can call you up for no reason and ask for repayment immediately. Their practical method of enforcing their request is to bounce any cheque issued in future. It is a rare and extreme course of action. You should not worry unduly about this, but it is a warning about putting too much reliance on an overdraft to fund the business.

The length of the repayment of loans is very much negotiable. Some loans last for two years, some for ten. Some are repayable equally over the life of the loan. For others, repayment can be negotiated to start from, say, two years and to be paid equally over the balance of the loan. Loans exist which require payment of interest only, with no capital repayment.

The rule of thumb about loan repayments is that loans should be repaid no later than expiry of the asset the loan is funding. A loan which funds property can last for ten to twenty years. A loan to fund a car should be paid back within, say, three years. Generally, if part of a loan is needed for longer than the life of the asset, there is a good chance it should be funded by equity, not by loan.

There are two problems – and solutions – with this evaluation. Firstly, working capital. Stock and debtors last between two to six months. Part of the working capital will be funded by creditors with a similar life expectancy. Of the balance, some will expire within the short time frame, but the balance is core debt and capital which will continue throughout any time the company has its present level of business. The 'core' element should be funded by equity or long-term loans. The balance should be funded by short-term borrowings. Since these short-term borrowings usually take the form of an overdraft, it is worthwhile negotiating a six-month period with the bank to stop them calling in the debt within, say, six months of giving notice.

The second problem is identifying which funding relates to which asset. With loans and capital of £500,000 each, for example, much of the loan should be allocated to equipment to establish what equity is funding. The trick is to turn the problem on its head. List the projected assets and identify the ideal funding. Establish the amount of short-term loans and the amount and length of longer-term loans. Compare those with facilities in place and renegotiate, if appropriate.

Summary

In summary, the advantage of loans is that the shareholders maintain their share of the company. The disadvantages are that interest charges are made, which reduce the company's profits. And the loan must be repaid, which means funds must be made available in future which would otherwise be available for the company to use or for distribution to its shareholders.

Investment Attributes Of Equity

Attributes

The main feature of raising equity funding is that the shareholders release some form of stake they have in the company. That stake is probably transferable by the new shareholder to anyone chosen by that shareholder.

Equity takes a long time to raise. There are usually colossal professional costs involved. There are onerous legal burdens which need to be complied with when raising equity, particularly so when raising finance from the general public.

Cost

The cost of obtaining equity does not usually affect the profit figure. It increases the value of the company. The cost, however, is a reduced share in the value of the company. The traditional evaluation of the 'price' of raising equity is established by comparing the value of full ownership at the present level of trading with the value of a reduced share of a larger, more valuable business. This evaluation is then compared with the respective values if borrowings fund expansion instead of equity. For example, a 100% shareholding of the present company could be between £7–10 million. However, 75% of the grown company could be projected at £12–15 million. This should be compared with owning 100% of the company funded by borrowings, with reduced profits, to pay interest. The value of the company could be 100% of £9–13 million. The 'saving' from borrowing is compared with the risk (and effect) of the company performing worse than expected. Similarly, the directors would evaluate the reduced room for manoeuvre if the business out-turn was worse than expected, given that there would now be less security available for borrowing compared with raising equity.

Availability

The availability of equity depends on the perceived attraction of the issue to an investor. This comes about by the investor comparing the rate of return he expects with the risk of losing some or all of that money. The product of 'attractiveness' is then compared with other opportunities which exist at the same time. As a consequence, the availability depends on the state of the economy. In short, availability of equity funding is very uncertain.

Comparing advantages with disadvantages

Equity is usually not repayable. Once cash has been injected into the company, it is available forever. There is no interest charge to depress profits. However, existing shareholders reduce their shares of that company.

For new shareholders to invest money in the company, they must believe the return will exceed the loss of interest from having those funds in a bank deposit. This means they believe the cost to existing shareholders will be more if equity is injected, than if the money were borrowed from the bank.

Equity is therefore particularly suitable to fund a risk venture (one where money is spent without buying an asset which retains an equivalent value). It is also suitable for funding very long-term assets, core working capital or any other funding which cannot be funded by a bank.

Choosing between the sources

Once the amount and length of the funding the company is likely to need has been projected, and the value of the security within the company's (or outside) assets has been counted, the 'equity' decision can be made. The planner will need to:

1 Estimate the value of the company without expansion, in two to five years.
2 Estimate the value of the company with expansion, if all additional funding needs are satisfied by borrowings.
3 Estimate the value of the reduced shareholding in the company on the basis of the above, but assuming all additional funds are injected by equity.

This provides a guide about the 'cost' of funding growth by equity. The benefits of equity must be evaluated by reference to the risk evaluation discussed in Chapters 13 and 14. When projections are made on the basis of reduced, and increased, achievements, the alternate funding needs are evaluated. Work out, realistically, how additional funds would be raised if you were presently in the 'revised projection' circumstances. Evaluate how easy or difficult raising the funds would be. Note particularly the speed with which funds would be needed. There is nothing to stop you discussing these contingencies with your bank to try to gauge how they would react if this occurred. It may be helpful to take professional advice on this.

It is both the availability of borrowings in these circumstances, and the effect of the additional cost, that needs to be considered. Each time, compare the value of the company which raised equity with that which borrowed additional funds. Remember that an underfunded company is worth proportionally less than a better-funded company in times of trouble. However, the preferred balance between risk and return is a very personal matter and will vary from almost any company to any advisor. The end result of the detailed evaluation will probably bring you to the 'conventional' view on equity, which is – equity should fund risk.

Assets which have a value in themselves can be funded by borrowings, taking proper account of assets which depreciate in value. This is subject to a company's ability to pay interest and repay the loan from retained profits. If there is a risk of assets loss, or there is a risk of profits being unable to fund interest and loan repayment, equity should be provided.

In addition, it is always prudent to obtain 'buffer' equity to provide a cushion for contingency if things go wrong, or simply to be used to exploit gross opportunities which are, as yet, unplanned. The type of organizations and entities that make funding available were set out above. Finding the right organization from within each category requires research.

Once the amount and length of the funding the company is likely to need has been projected, and the value of the security within the company's (or outside) assets has been counted, the 'equity' decision can be made.

Chapter Summary

- Most funding can be divided into three sources. These are trade credit, loans and equity.
- Trade credit tends to be cheap, but the availability and amount of credit can vary uncontrollably.
- Loans tend to have an interest cost. The cost is usually variably and, as such, difficult to predict. But the cost can also be fixed in certain circumstances. There is a limited availability of loans and it is a form of funding that can be withdrawn without agreement of management.
- Equity is usually more expensive to shareholders than any other form of finance – but it is usually free to the company. The availability and cost to shareholders varies enormously from company to company. The cost of raising equity tends to be high. The effect on control of the company can be substantial if the 50% shareholding passes from one group of investors to another.

- Choosing between the sources of funding requires evaluation of the nature of funding required, the cost to the company and the shareholder, and the availability of funding. It is a complex evaluation which usually requires the assistance of professional advisors.

Part   4

Focusing the Plan

13 Risk

'We had lent the company £2 million last year. They were projecting a loss of £400,000 for the year and profits of £1 million next year. All the funding was in place. But they spent £400,000 too much on their office extension. If only they had told us in advance. If only.'

They say what distinguishes man from animal is the ability to understand concepts. It allows language and foresight. It links experience of using a sharp stone with the problem of how to cut something open. It links the cause of fire with the effect – allowing its control. The thought process creates tools and shelter. The process enables us to work out the result of an action in advance of that action.

This brain power created society and economy. It allowed us to farm and build. It allows us, even today, to improve on existing techniques by inventing new methods and machines. It created the concept of a business entity and is fundamental in controlling business development.

From an evolutionary perspective, Business Planning is the facility of projecting what could happen in certain circumstances and preventing some of the less desired possibilities by taking appropriate action in advance. This is the process that created the industrial revolution – the development of new techniques to produce more for less. It was not simply the ability to make machines that slung the world into the twentieth century. It was the ability to harness the knowledge and to manage to organize the transition of society to fulfil the potential that created the success of industry. With of all the things that could have gone wrong with the business development, it was only the people with the foresight and ability to deal with the problems that reaped the rewards.

And here we are, with an even more momentous slinging action in progress, ready to rocket into the twenty-first century. We are in the adolescent stages of the 'microchip' era. History is repeating itself. It is not the technological knowhow that develops the business – it is its harnessing. The microchip era will become more significant to mankind not because of some clever scientists, but because business managers, like you, can take advantage, either directly or by using services or goods that exploit improved methods. The successful will reap the benefits. The failures will be heard of no more. And success requires that all the problems that could arise be dealt with.

Some problems can be dealt with at the time they arise. If a secretary is ill, reorganizing the work schedule into its correct priority may be all that is needed. But many problems are insoluble once they have arisen. It is too late to discover that a market for a new product does not exist if it is left until after the capital expenditure has been spent or committed. It is these types of problems that a Business Plan must deal with.

This chapter deals with Risk. After the Plan has been designed, the crucial task of identifying what can go wrong starts. You need to identify what could go wrong, how likely it is to go wrong and the financial consequence of it happening. And if necessary, you must identify what you would do if it were to happen. If done properly, this review is very likely to throw out a modification to the original Plan. You may reduce capital expenditure or raise additional funding. You may tinker with target markets or supply sources. Or you may decide the risk of certain events could be so devastating to the business, you could not afford to embark on the Plan for fear of total failure.

Background to Risk

When planning a business, the first aspect of the Plan dealt with is what you expect to happen. When the full financial consequences are understood, the next stage is to evaluate what could happen if things do not go according to plan. Before you start to implement the Plan, it is important to know what could happen. Where a particular outcome would be unacceptable. you should devise a contingency Plan to ensure the end result of the business will still fall within the company's overall objectives. Is there any specific cash outlay or commitment which creates this risk? If so, can the cost be delayed until the risk has become less likely to occur? If nothing can be done, you should consider how likely it is that the problem outcome will occur. If it is high, you should weigh up whether the potential benefits sufficiently compensate for the potentially devastating risk. If so, it is worth trying to arrange to adopt a position to reduce the impact of the risk to manageable proportions. The key to doing this successfully is to identify the risk in the first place.

You should also consider what you would do in a few months time if it became apparent your worst fears were realized. If you would take specific action to minimize or contain the problem, this should be incorporated within a contingency Plan.

Identifying risk

When planning a business, you must first plan for what you expect. When the full financial consequences are understood, the next stage is to evaluate what could happen if things do not go according to plan. Before you start to implement the Plan, it is important to know the effect of deviating from it. Where a particular outcome would be unacceptable, you should take any steps possible to neutralize or minimize the effect of the risk. This may involve devising a contingency Plan to ensure the end result of the business is steered back to fall within the overall objectives. If none of this is possible, you need to consider how likely it is that this outcome could occur.

If the likelihood is high, you should consider whether any particular commitment or outlay is responsible. You then need to weigh up whether the potential benefits are sufficient to warrant taking this risk. If so, it is still worth trying to protect the company against or to eliminate the risk or its effect. There may be steps that can be taken now. Perhaps they will be incorporated into the final Plan, which modify both the potential profits and also the potential downside cost. Perhaps the steps will not be taken until it is known that the risk problem is likely to happen. In this case, a contingency Plan should be devised.

The risks involved in Business Planning become clearer when you consider what is required of you when planning. You must:

- Create an idea for growth that will work.
- Forecast how well it will work for the next three to five years.
- Forecast how many people will be needed to work.
- Specify in which month those people will be taken on.
- Forecast interest rates and inflation in each of the next 60 months.
- Estimate overheads based on the level of activities.
- Predict tax rates.
- State how much funding is needed and when it will be repaid.
- Forecast exchange rates (if relevant).
- Forecast how quickly the economy will grow and recede.
- Forecast how quickly your industry will grow and recede.
- Project the effect of competitors, existing and those yet to arrive.

Since expert economic analysts predict the economy about as accurately as weather forecasters predict next week's weather, these aspects of Business Planning are prone to error. There are a hundred things that can happen unexpectedly in running a business. It is often referred to, succinctly, as 'Risk'. It is a fact of life that must be dealt with.

Companies may consider many techniques to cope with risk. Where relevant, they would incorporate any results in the Plan. Examples of risk avoidance actions are as follows:

- Interest rates varying — hedge the loan or match the cost with income.
- Exchange rates varying — hedge the foreign currency position or match costs with income.
- Too few suppliers — increase the supply base; diversify areas of activity.
- Too few customers — increase selling activities; change pricing structure; expand product range; buy out competitors.
- Excessive competition — buy our competitors; increase own efficiency; improve sales effectiveness.
- Using more funds than expected — spend less now; delay capital expenditure program; improve debt collection procedures; reduce stock levels; arrange contingency funding.
- Sales missing target — not specific enough risk.

- Margins missing target   – improve marketing; improve buying performance; change target market; shelve expansion plans which require high initial expenditure.

Affordable risk

The main concern of missing target is the financial consequence. Once a risk has been identified, the effect needs to be explored by reworking the forecasts to show what would happen if the risk occurred. Ironically, preforming better than planned can have almost the same effect as doing worse, at least in the short run. The effect on profits and cash flow arises when there is a deviation from projected profits or from projected cash flow. Or both. At the planning stage, the key problem to be resolved is, 'How likely is a shortfall to occur, how much is the shortfall liable to be and can the business cope if this happens?'

Some risks may be negligible. The possibility of business interruption from power cuts, for example, is not significant because the supply is reliable and because alternate supply could be found in an emergency. Contrast that with exactly the same situation in 1985 when Arthur Scargill announced a miners' strike. It was uncertain whether there would be power interruptions. The risk had to be evaluated. It would almost certainly have affected a decision to build a power generator at the time. It would probably not, however, have altered a decision to exploit an overseas market to a company with direct access to a nuclear power station.

If the business can cope with the risk, or the likelihood of it happening is so remote, then you may proceed. It might be worthwhile trying to eliminate the risk, as discussed above. But if the business would do so badly that it would collapse, or be forced to sell out, or if management would be forced out by shareholders or the bank, the business could not afford to take the risk. Unless, that is, you are prepared to accept that outcome.

A business can never eliminate risk. But it is the duty of management to know what the stakes are and how high the risk is. Then the decisions can be made.

Summary

- The planning process must deal with the possibility of failing to achieve targets.
- To deal with this risk requires identifying the ways in which this can occur and quantifying the financial consequence of each type of failure. The overall risk then needs to be compared with the reward of taking the risk in the first place.
- You should place special weighting on whether the business can afford the risk. The consequences of missing some targets in some circumstances are so severe that the business could not afford to take the risk without collapsing at the end. If this is a possibility, serious consideration should be given to fundamentally changing the Plan to avoid this possibility.

14   Handling Risk

'The challenge for a Business Plan is to provide as clear a picture of the non-financial aspects of a business as the five-year summaries give of its financial performance.'

Chess is a game which almost personifies certain aspects of a Business Plan. It is one of the oldest games. Playing it involves setting out a game plan, planning your next moves and judging the opponent's most likely response. If moves happen which you have not anticipated, the plan may require modification. Since there are several possible moves that your opponent can make, you may choose a move which, whilst being less dynamic, is less likely to leave you open to counter-attack. You may, on the other hand, push for a quicker and glorious victory.

There must be elements of enjoyment in the mental challenge of the Business Planning process. The shame is that the outcome is gambled upon – the stakes are the amount of money invested, committed or locked up in the business. It is a costly exercise to lose.

As with the game, the Plan for the business can be more or less risky. This chapter sets out ways of containing the risk within acceptable levels.

Measuring the risk

The key to dealing with risk is to have a clear understanding of what the risk is. This requires some form of measurement. The first step is to identify all risk areas, and then to evaluate the likelihood of each. This includes evaluating the possible scale of problems, considering how the business would react to the event and what the cost would be.

The downside risk then needs to be compared with the likelihood and benefits of the Plan succeeding. The result of this evaluation is frequently a modification of the original

Plan, or a series of insurance or contingency Plans. The companies which do not perform this type of evaluation are usually the ones unprepared and unable to cope if targets start to fall.

No-one says a business should not take a risk. But financiers, and those with common sense, say you should not take risks you cannot afford. They mean, specifically, those risks other than the ones you are virtually certain will not take place. You may be virtually certain interest rates will not rise to 30% within the next three years, but an increase back to 15% cannot be ruled out, even if that level is not expected by any economic forecasters at present. The important point to consider is, 'How likely is this to occur, and if it does, what is the effect?'.

Business Plan Technique for Dealing with Risk

The technique for dealing with risk is a methodical recalculation of the effect on profits and cash flow of different outcomes of the Plan. Many businesses fall into the trap of simply recalculating the figures as if it were an arithmetic exercise. Whereas this may be interesting, the key to the successful Plan is devising a company reaction in the event that each considered outcome could arise. And then recomputing the figures.

Profit Risk

Firstly, consider Sales volumes. By this stage, the full profit and cash flow models will have been set out. Recalculate the effect on profits and funding if sales volumes were to fall by, say, 10%. Be realistic. Take account of the time lag before you are likely to become aware the shortfall is likely, and the time it takes for the remedies to come through. The point of the revision is not to test how well a spreadsheet works; it is to think of the likely actions in the circumstances and to rework the Plan in full. It should take substantially less time than the original Plan, but quite a lot longer than simply changing the sales figure in an otherwise unamended spreadsheet.

If the size of the sales force would be increased, for example, to make up the lost sales, reflect this. If the number of telephone calls and travel to potential customers were to reduce, reflect it. If after four months, you were likely to reduce the sales team to compensate for the lower volume of sales, reflect this.

Carry out a full, realistic review, and project profits and funding requirements at that level. Then recalculate the model on the basis of, say, a 20% drop. Then, say, a 30% drop. The different levels of possible drop would depend on the possibility of these occurring. In practice, the bands should be calculated on the basis of the level of drop you would consider to be:

- Expected
- Lowest band in range of expected
- Sales if things were really bad
- Sales if things were disastrous
- Sales at an almost inconceivable level

The evaluation should go upwards as well as downwards. Firstly, it gives an encouraging counterbalance to pessimism. Secondly, since growth requires funding, the cash requirements may increase if the company outperforms the Plan. The consequence of this review may be to change the balance of funding sought between borrowings and equity. It may also warn of actions that are too risky to warrant the rewards that could be achieved, and may result in the company redirecting its Plan. If it does, there is a good chance you are succeeding in planning your business.

Going upwards on the evaluation usually requires less steps and usually covers a smaller range since improved performance occurs less often than a reduced outcome.

Once the process is complete, you may have a table that looks like this:

Table 14.1 **Profit risk**

a) Profit and loss account
   Year ending 30 September 1992

	£'000	£'000	£'000
Turnover	1,604	1,440	1,230
Gross profits	682	610	530
Overheads	616	574	512
Net profits	66	36	18

Year ending 30 September 1993

Turnover	1,780	1,600	1,335
Gross profits	765	688	590
Overheads	649	605	540
Net profits	116	83	50

b) Cash flow funding

Fixed assets required	150	150	150
Working capital surplus (minimum)	175	127	86
Net loans/overdrafts (max. level forecast)	(65)	(83)	(131)

Then consider, in turn, the following assumptions. Each time the assumption is changed, keep all other assumptions identical to the expected Plan. Change only the aspects of the Plan that would be amended in the event of the tested variation:

- Variation in production/purchase costs.
- The effect of reduction in sales prices to stimulate additional demand. Assume, for each price change, two or three possible volume changes. Increase the range of possible outcomes the less certain you are about the outcome. Also consider the effect of increase in sales prices with the consequent reduction in volumes and overheads.
- Disruption to supplies, both from suppliers and to customers.

- Variations in any key overhead. These are sometimes considered together. They usually include: salaries; cost of premises; marketing; interest.

Sometimes overheads are considered as a whole, with different inflation rates considered. As with each consideration, calculate the effect on all other aspects of the forecast resulting from each variation. Remember, for example, to vary purchase costs and sales prices, with inflationary increases, but not if overheads exceed target as a result of needing to employ more staff than anticipated.

A disadvantage of 'lumping together' overheads is the difficulty of considering realistically the different risks, and the effect on other aspects of the business of a change in one of the assumptions. As a 20% increase in the number of personnel can affect rent, telephone costs, travel and many other cost factors, it is a good example of a cost that should be evaluated separately.

For each of the assumptions mentioned above, there may be a hundred other possible problems. Look carefully at the company's activities to identify all possible problems. If the potential problem is real, evaluate it.

Asset/Liability Risk

The next series of evaluations look at assumptions relating to assets and liabilities. The same principles apply. The basic Plan should be used as the basis. Each assumption should be considered in turn to quantify the effect on cash requirements and profits. Once the effect is known, you are able to evaluate how likely each outcome, or combination of outcomes, is to occur. With all the numbers at your finger tips, the real risk evaluation is as simple as it gets. Typical risks to consider are:

- Variation in the level of fixed assets and equipment. Remember to consider the entire model with each possible variation. If additional equipment is needed, cash flow requirements directly increase. Indirectly, interest costs and depreciation also increase, along with any other related costs such as the size of premises, handling costs and other related overheads.
- Variation in the level of stock holdings. As the level of stock increases, do not forget to allow for the effect on increased sales, if appropriate, increased storage and interest costs and increased cost of stock obsolescence and deterioration.
- Variations in the length of time debtors take to pay. If the business grows quickly, or if the Plan takes the company into new areas of customer or product base, it is sensible to review the effect of the collection period increasing by 30 days or even as much as 60 days. Also remember to include the contingency increase in the cost of debt collection and bad debts as debtors increase in value.
- If the company has any other assets, possible variations in these should also be considered if large enough to be significant.
- Variations in the length of time taken to pay creditors. If the Company were able to negotiate increases in payment time to suppliers, the effect should be quantified. Conversely, if the company is taking longer to pay suppliers than contracted, a review should be carried out to consider the effect of reducing payment times.

Remember to include the gain from taking payment discounts if these are available.

Interpreting the Results

The final series of evaluations are the fun ones. With the models in place, and with the results, they need interpreting. By the time you get to this stage, there will be a substantial number of results, plotted in simple tables. The overall Plan must now be revisited. The terms of the review are simple. Is the Plan still the best route for the company? The possible problems have been identified and quantified. The proposed action has been devised in the event of deviation of actual performance from the Plan. The costs and likelihood of the various possibilities are reviewed to confirm whether the Plan still meets the objectives of the business in the long term. If specific risks are too high or costly, the Plan may be modified or amended to improve its thrust, if relevant. The final review, therefore, evaluates the effect of ideas you have to avoid excessive risks identified above. It includes reconsidering the effect of increasing the marketing budget, changing the basis of marketing, combining several operating units into one, selling off part of the business and any other business development ideas which are seriously proposed.

There are three things to note about the final review. Firstly, each variation needs to be considered only if the result could be significant. If you are unsure, carry out the evaluation. Often the results of other possible outcomes can be guessed from the first. It may save time.

Secondly, note again this is not a mechanical exercise to keep accountants happy, or the Financial Director unhappy. Each variation requires careful consideration. In particular, it is fundamental to identify how the company would react if the tested outcome were the reality and to incorporate any costs and benefits in the test. It helps the company to react quicker at a later date if it becomes necessary.

Thirdly, the evaluations above will take a massive amount of time to complete. The Business Plan document can have the appearance of being complete without these evaluations. But the Plan itself may be wrong. Further, the absence of contingency planning is usually apparent when financiers discuss details of the Plan at a later date. Avoiding this evaluation is an unwise short cut. The good news, however, is that no-one ever carried out as comprehensive an evaluation as described above. Many of the results are either predictable or insignificant. However, each point should be considered, even if the full model revision is excessive.

It is difficult to provide a general summary of interpreting results since they are so varied. Every company will have different strengths and weaknesses and the results mean different things to different people. For this exercise, experience or expert advice can be invaluable. But there are a few points common to all business which help:

- It is imperative to be clear about the long-term objectives of the business. If the company requires sustained, long-term growth, it may sacrifice short-term profits to achieve it. If the company aims to obtain a stock exchange listing shortly, it may prefer diversification.

- Many businesses fail from inadequate funding. If the cost of expansion is to expose the company to vastly inadequate funding, if failure to meet targets are foreseeable, either slower growth may achieve better results than planned growth or more funding may be raised than initially needed. The point is to deal with weak areas of the Plan either by adapting the Plan or arranging contingency actions or facilities in the event of a problem. Once the Plan has commenced, it is usually impossible to go back to the position you were at before you started once targets have failed to be met.
- If Directors have not experienced the new size company, after growth, their ability to predict the outcome will inevitably be impaired. In these circumstances, ensure the range of possible outcomes of each variation should be large. Appropriate weighting should be given to the effect of possible error in forecasts.
- If risks are considered to be uncomfortably high, identify which areas are most prone to risk and try to reduce those specific risks. If interest rates are critical, consider fixed rate loans. If salaries are critical, consider an element of performance-related pay. If the debt payment period is critical, consider factoring debts or introducing a pricing policy to discourage slow payments.
- Always consider radical alternatives. Even if they are irrelevant, they may inspire an unorthodox solution to a problem. Consider, for example, eliminating a product range or launching a substantial advertising campaign.
- If a company is not profitable before growth, it is rarely profitable after growth, despite the theory of improved performance from spreading overheads. In these circumstances, pay particularly close attention to possible shortfalls from expectations. Nothing requires a company to grow. In practice, if a company grows when it has problems, it is usually the problems that grow, not the profits.
- Timing is important in growth, especially if a business is cyclical. Consideration should be given to delaying or speeding up the date of commencement of the Plan.
- Raising finance always costs time and money. Both should be taken into account in forecasting, particularly if either are critical. If targets are not met, remember to include the time and costs involved in dealing with this aspect of the business when evaluating the effect on costs.

Chapter Summary

- The key to dealing with risk is understanding it. This means identifying how the actual trading results could deviate from the Plan and quantifying the financial effect of each.
- The evaluation requires a methodical recalculation of different outcomes. It is more than an arithmetic exercise. It only works properly if you incorporate into the forecasts how you would react to specific events if they occurred in practice. If less staff would be employed, for example, were turnover to fall by more than 20%, and this was a real possibility, the evaluation should account for the lower level of staff at the time that the staff levels would be lower than originally forecast.

- The effect of variations both on profits and on the level of funding needed must be considered separately.
- Once the recalculations are complete, they should be summarized in a simple table.
- Then the original Plan should be reconsidered. Taking account of the expected benefits, are the risks worth taking? Or can the Plan be modified to keep most of the benefits whilst reducing many of the more extreme risks? Once the final evaluation is complete, the final Plan is adopted.

Part 5

What the Users Think

15　Investors

'Does the company or group really know what its function is? In practice, I will only get to see that from the Plan.'

This series of chapters summarizes a number of meetings held with readers of Business Plan documents. It is important to understand the psychology of the other side to a negotiation if you are to arrange the most appropriate (best) deal possible. It also helps to know how to phrase the parts of the Plan that address their concerns or desires.

When you are selling or negotiating something important, it is almost inconceivable that you would not find out as much as you could about the 'opposition'. The more you know about your adversary, the more successful you are likely to be. Raising funds for your business is akin to selling not just some products, but the whole operation: to fund not just a couple of transactions, but a whole new tranche of business. The more you know about the other side, the better.

Almost all investors and bankers would be upset to think of themselves as being 'on the other side'. They all believe, rightly, that they are as much part of a business they lend to or invest in as any other participator. They have specific skills and useful advice that can be particularly valuable if used in the right spirit. The conflicting interests occur before they have invested, or at the time they are being asked to lend more.

One chapter in the series summarizes a legal view of Business Planning as it affects the planner. It gives an interesting cautionary tone to an otherwise positive business activity. This chapter gives feedback from investors about what they like and dislike about Plans they see.

Background

There is a vast, sophisticated market for Investment money. Investment funds of several million pounds are raised many times each year. Each fund is set up with a different purpose. Some are set up to invest exclusively in property, some in new business, some in new technology. Some funds like risk, others hate it. Each fund is different. You should know which fund you are approaching before asking them to consider your Plan. There is no point in a technology company asking a retail fund to consider investing in it. Each fund is controlled by different people. Each fund manager has a different view on what makes a good proposition, or a good management team.

But for every view that is different, it is surprising how many views are shared. Interviews were set up with four people responsible for deciding on where to invest these funds.

London Venture Capitalist

The first interview was with the founder of the venture capital subsidiary of a merchant bank. He had spent a number of years in America, bringing back with him the latest investment techniques of the mid-eighties. Funds have been raised specifically for European-wide ventures. The company has no preference for specific industry. Their management style is 'hands on'. They will only invest in business where they can provide the added value of management expertise in their chosen field. His observations on Business Plans were interesting.

The purpose of a Plan, he believes, is to set out a financial proposal. It allows management to dream dreams, creating a road map for the future which management can follow. He says he can tell a business which has an effective Plan, because everyone throughout the whole organization knows what the company's aim is, and what their role is within the whole.

When he sees a Plan, he is looking primarily at whether the group can articulate what it is trying to do. If it is not clear or well articulated, it is indicative of management's inability to communicate generally – which is indicative of inadequate management skills. If management is unable to write a business 'road map', it doesn't deserve to be in business. It can be just two pages. He wants to be able to say, 'I see what they want to do'.

He prefers companies to have an aggressive stance towards potential shareholders. There are a few things he wants them to articulate clearly. He likes Plans which say 'This is what we are looking for. There is 25% of the company up for grabs. This is what it costs. Are you interested?' He is particularly keen that they are also clear about the quality of money they are looking for. What sort of shareholders do they want? Do they want ones with a particular expertise, desired contacts, management skills? Or do they want ones who will just inject money with no questions asked? They should have specific criteria and a list of potential investors. He does not want to invest in a company which has not done enough homework on what they want, since it almost always leads to problems with the relationship later on.

When looking at a proposal, he puts a high emphasis on the group's positioning. It is a key word for him. It suggests the market sector a company is operating in and how the group interacts with its competition. The Strategy is the key to the Plan. He would prefer to see a company bicycling in the right direction than a Rolls Royce driving in the wrong one.

'Do they know what the function of their business is?' He means by that, do they know the real value of their products or service? They must have an awareness of the sales per product and, more importantly, the cost per product. The cost of making each unit of medical equipment must, for example, include the cost of administration, and the cost of running an airline must be in terms of costs per passenger miles travelled. This perception only exists where there are good management skills. It is essential to controlling the costs and margins of a business. Management without the right experience will not be able to evaluate the functional aspects of the Plan properly. And when he invests, he believes he is buying experience.

The amount of information he expects to see about the market depends on how unusual the product is. There is not much to say about a construction company, for example, which is not already self-evident. He would expect them to concentrate more on the 'cost battle' with competitors. Conversely, if a product is rarefied, the Plan should look at who is providing the function now and compare the industry with yours.

He is looking for the section on competition to demonstrate that the company's product has a significantly lower cost to customers than that of its competitors, or a better quality for the same cost – and that the advantage is secure over, say, the next three years. He expects to see a list of competitors, which pose a specific threat and how much competition the competitors would be able to cope with. 'Thinking about these things in the right terms is more important than the Plan itself,' he says.

He turns down about 98% of proposals and says it is very rare that he is left with the impression 'Boy, that was good!' after reading a Plan. Most are too long and have too many financials – none of which are believable anyway. He doesn't even read the Plan if it has the Accountant's name on the front. He wants to read what the management are capable of, and how articulate they are. If the Plan is technically poor, he falls back on whether he believes in these people. If he originally thought they were ordinary, a technically badly written Plan will usually be enough for him to say no.

The best Plans are the ones that deteriorate most rapidly into work. They set out clearly what will happen if funds are raised – from tomorrow morning. Too often, they are theoretical documents, without an Action Plan. He contrasts this with a Plan that has too much urgency. There can be no good Plan that will not work if implemented in, say, three months' time. If the company must have money today, he would probably turn it down for having got into this position in the first place.

Chris Curry – The Piper Trust

The Piper Trust is an independent investment fund. The managers of the fund all have direct management experience. The fund specializes in investing in the retail sector. As proof of its capabilities, the fund boasts to have been successful even during the retail recession of 1989 to 1991 – reputed to have been one of the worst recessions for the industry for decades. The funds will only invest in companies that are open to advice from Piper and that may manifest itself through a direct management involvement, or simply be limited to participation at board meetings if that is all that is required.

'I see about two hundred Business Plans a year. They range from clear, concise and exciting to long, rambling and dull. The Business Plan is usually the first contact a venture capitalist has with an investment proposition and maybe for four out of five it will be the last. So it is vital it is user friendly, clear and concise.

'For a Plan to be user friendly it must be physically user friendly. Something that is easy to read without pages falling out and piles of loose paper flying everywhere. "Clear" means it must be well structured. It must contain an executive summary, a contents page and all the elements required in a Business Plan in a logical format. "Concise" means containing sufficient to be able to make an initial judgement but not ending up with a time sufficient to put off even the most interested reader.

'In very simple terms, in my mind, there are three hurdles that a plan has to jump. Firstly, the validity of the business idea. This is generally more difficult to judge in a start-up or early stage proposition. The validation can be achieved through market analysis, market research and historic information – and more simply, by answering the question from the customer's point of view, "Is there a need for this business?"

'The second hurdle is the management team. The Plan must demonstrate management's experience, particularly its relevant experience, and its ability to implement the Plan. This includes the way it will work as a team, any history of this, and how and when the team will be expanded. The area of judgement of the people involved in a Plan is the most difficult when assessing an investment opportunity and will obviously be based on more than just the Plan. But first impressions will be formed at this stage and it is therefore a vital element.

'The third hurdle is the commercial viability of the business. It needs to be clear that the business can make an economic return based on reasonable assumptions. Those assumptions need to be founded on reality and how they were arrived at is important. Obviously, if there is historic financial information against which the projections can be compared it is important to include this. Although it may eventually be necessary to have produced every detailed sensitivity analysis and monthly forecasts for five years, including every financial detail possible in a first Plan is normally a waste and can often put people off. I would say that a clear summary is essential.

'If a Plan ever gets over these hurdles, then it is worth me meeting the management team – so in the first instance this is the objective of the Plan.

'As a final note, from reading a Business Plan you can often get a good sense of the writer's interest and excitement about the business. This can be important in taking it to the next stage. If the Plan is written by non-management such as a consultant or advisor, generally there is none of that feeling. You can always tell when this happens. Management should always write the Plan themselves.'

John Bridges – Keith Bailey Rogers

Keith Bailey Rogers are a firm of stockbrokers, with a growing Corporate Finance department. The firm has remained an independent partnership and has been in existence for over a century. They have three key functions: one is to raise capital for developing businesses; another is to float companies on the Stock Exchange; a third is involvement in all aspects of mergers and acquisitions of companies.

'I see on average two or three Plans every day. Some are good, some are bad. I have a simple motto – the more glossy the Plan, the worse the proposition.

'One of the first things I look at is the CV of the people involved. To me, it is even more important than the deal or the product. I want to know who the people are behind the proposals – their backgrounds, their career paths relevant to what they are trying to do – to get a general feel about their suitability for the job. I will wait to get them before reviewing a Plan where they are missing.

'The best Plans are the ones that are simple and straight to the point. They should be easily understandable and easily readable. I don't want to waste time ploughing through weighty documents to read something that could be said as well in two pages.

'The worst Plan I read was expensively produced, by a high-tech company. It was the sort of product that would mystify anyone. I found it difficult to understand the market. It had more than one hundred pages, with few sub-headings or paragraphs to break up the text. The product may have been very good. All other aspects of the Plan may have been good. But the whole thing was an indigestible mess.

'There are aspects of a good product that stick out like a sore thumb. The product fulfils an easily identifiable need in the marketplace. Therefore, the Plan should identify the need well, and why the product is needed in the marketplace. There is a balance between being verbiage and concisensss. The clearer the Plan is, the more pleasant it is to read. But if the Plan is too long, the point often fails to be made forcefully enough.

'The market size is a key aspect of the Plans I look at. The description should be no more than two pages long. If no data exist to support the estimation of the market size, that should not substitute for the need to get the message across.

'My overall impressions about Business Plans comes from one of the first adages I was introduced to – KISS . . . Keep It Simple Stupid.'

Susan Hayes – formerly Salomon Brothers Inc

Susan Hayes began in her career at Salomon Brothers Venture Capital in 1986. The Venture group has a US$40 million fund, most of which is invested in small, private start-up situations in the high-technology, medical and environmental areas. Susan's primary focus was the medical arena. She has since left and moved on to video and photography.

'I find Business Plans to be pretty straightforward. They usually follow a basic format with each bit of information falling into a logical sequence. I don't really care about the "how" if you don't tell me the "what" first. When they don't follow a formula, a red light goes on in my head and I wonder if information was left out on purpose or if these people simply just don't know. Either way, I'm sceptical and proceed with caution.

'In a good Plan, the first paragraph should tell me what the company does, what it's products or services are, who the target market is, what size the overall market is and what portion of market share they plan to obtain – and how. I want to know right up front how much money they are looking for, how far it will take them, and how much has already gone in. I want to know who the other investors are, if the investors are well-known names, people who have made money in the past. I give the Business Plan a close read. Basically, I want them to tell me why I should consider this investment. "Convince me!" From all this information, I can usually determine if I want to do any "due diligence" or if I should call them and say that we're not interested.

'A poorly written Plan is one that is "slim" on information. If it doesn't answer all my obvious questions in the first few minutes of reading, they lose my attention. I don't have time to read through three chapters to find out what they do. Get to the point, don't give me fluff!

'Regardless of how complex the technology is, a lay person should be able to understand, or at least get a good idea of, what the product or service does. If the company writing the Plan uses a lot of fancy terms thinking it will impress the reader, they're often mistaken. The reader wants to know in the most basic terms, What does it do and why?

'Usually I find that when information is missing, nine times out of ten it's the competition. I find that either the management team hasn't truly identified who their competitors are or the competitors are such large household names that they've been left out on purpose so as not to frighten the venture capitalist off. Either way, it's not an ideal situation. I would rather they tell me what I'm up against right from the start. If, through due diligence, I discover that the company's biggest competitor is a large, Fortune 1000 company and it's obvious, I lose faith in the management team. That alone would justify tossing the deal in the waste basket.

'A strong management team is critical for any start-up company. Most venture capitalists would rather back an excellent team (an 'A' team) with a good product over an excellent product with a good team (a 'B' team). We look for people who have years of knowledge in this particular industry, seasoned players with solid track records.

'Market? It's simple. Venture capitalists really only want to know . . . How big? How much? And how long?

'Generally, I find Business Plans a little flat and lifeless – like a Biology manual. I enjoy a bit of intrigue or humour now and then. Not slapstick but something clever, something that makes me think, keeps me on my toes – an interesting statistic, a future projection. It shows me that these people are savvy, that their Plan is well thought out.

'The bottom line? What is the exit strategy? How will the venture capitalist make money? That's all the venture capitalists care about . . . What's in it for me? A clever, well-executed Plan will make them aware of that pot of gold at the end of the rainbow. A smart Plan will present them with a platter of all the information they need to make that decision to move forward with the "due diligence" process. If you receive a call requesting more information, you've probably put together a good Plan, one that sparked some interest.

'Venture capitalists are a tough breed. They can be demanding, fussy and intolerant. But they read hundreds of Business Plans each week. I believe a Business Plan is like a novel. If the first two chapters are horrible, chances are, so is the rest.'

16   Bank Managers

'My main criticism of Plans is that they contain too much irrelevant information. I want to see how the business will work and how it will satisfy my requirements.'

Banks have different objectives from investors when they are looking at Business Plans. They are far less willing to take risk. The emphasis of a Plan aimed at banks needs redirecting from the investor-based Plan. But there is much of a bank's requirement that is the same as an investor's. Both seem to obtain comfort from the style, as a separate consideration from the content.

Several types of bankers were interviewed. Their perception and requirements of Business Plans are summarized below.

Gerard Gardner – Barclays Bank Plc

Gerard Gardner is the senior Corporate Manager at Barclays' prestigious Mayfair Business Centre. His portfolio includes the accounts of a number of major public and private companies and many medium-sized private organizations.

'I am often presented with a Business Plan which consists only of a budget, that is a profit forecast and cash flow forecast. We are actually looking for the Plan to reveal how the business is going to operate, who will operate it and what their objectives are for that business.

'Clients may be surprised when, at the first meeting, the budgets are initially put aside whilst we ask about the background of the company and its management. This may have been excluded from the Plan, but it is so helpful in understanding the figures.

'If it is absent, it is usually because the company thinks that the bank would not consider it relevant. But there is a risk that decisions may then be made based on misunderstandings and the message that the business wishes to communicate may not be received clearly.

'It can be difficult to judge how much supporting information is required within the text. For example, when discussing the marketplace and competition it is enough to convey an understanding of the market. Detailed technical reference may be unnecessary.

'To demonstrate this, we recently received an excellent Business Plan from an electronic components distribution company. Their market description stated little more than the percentage of the UK market they had, the percentage of the main franchise market that they have and the geographic location in which they sell. This was sufficient to give the reader an understanding of that aspect of the operation.

'Once we have an understanding of the background, then we can consider the figures in a more balanced way. It would be wrong to say that the text is just as important as the numbers. In truth, the numbers are more important, but the value of the numbers is diminished considerably in the absence of a text.

'The quality of Plans which are presented ranges from very good to very poor. And generally, the quality is better if there has been professional input. If the Company is in any doubt whether the Plan is adequate or incomplete, then they should take advice. This is particularly true when the Plan is intended to be the foundation of the Bank's lending decision and may subsequently be used as a means of measurement of performance.

'A poor Plan normally contains a number of recurring features. Amongst these is an absence of detail within the text which can often contain too much generalization. Frequently, cash flow forecasts reveal consistent improvement in bank balances with the elimination of borrowings at the end of the year. Whereas in reality, borrowings move both upwards and downwards at different times in the year, reflecting the seasonality inherent in most businesses. Profits are also shown as consistently rising. And it is important to view such a forecast with reference to knowledge of the industry and market in which the company is operating.

'There is no doubt that the submission of a poor Plan can serve to undermine the confidence of the Bank in the financial management of the business – whereas a good Plan can provide a better understanding of the business and inspire confidence. It also allows the Bank to make recommendations which might benefit the business.

'The key element in the production of a good Plan is understanding what the reader requires and then to keep it simple. If this is uncertain, professional advice should be taken.'

Rob Pike – National Westminster Bank Plc

Rob Pike is a Senior Manager at the Charing Cross Business Centre. He manages corporate customers with typical turnover in the £3 million to £30 million range.

'With a new business, the first thing I want to find out about is the individuals involved. I look at their business experience and management structure and the depth of the management team. Do they have the financial experience, as well as marketing and technical experience?

'Initially, I will scan view the Plan to get a feel for the business. You can easily tell if it took 3 hours or 30 hours to put together. For new proposals, given the number of Plans I look at, I need to be able to pull the good Plan from the bad, quickly. If no trouble has been taken, the Plan is rarely worth looking at in detail.

'I do not want seventy pages in the main body of the Plan, with all information the business can think of regurgitated, just to make it look impressive. Detail is needed but it should generally be included in the Appendices – I like to see comment on the basis the assumptions are made and I need the writer to be able to back up statement with fact or logic. I do not want to read that sales will grow by 30% if the market is declining and the writers have no idea how they will gain market share. The core Plan itself should ideally be no more than twenty pages. It should be about the people and their experience, products and the market, customers and competition, and of course funding requirements. The overview should be in the Plan. There should be a separate section for the financials. The detailed trading history, balance sheet and budgets should ideally be in the Appendix.

'Generally, I have an open mind when I get a Plan. I am easily put off if it looks scruffy, with little time or care taken. I am also put off if the Plan is really glossy. If so, it cannot be up to date. There is nothing I hate more than evaluating a Plan and being told afterwards that the information in the document has changed several times since it was prepared. It is such a waste of time for all concerned. You can learn a lot about the individual by the way the Plan is put together.

'A Business Plan is a route map. It is a map for the people running the business. And like any well-laid plan, it should have built in contingencies. If other people benefit from the Plan, such as bankers, investors or even suppliers, fine. But it is primarily for management. They must be prepared to check back at a later date that the company is still going in the right direction. The Plan should not be used just to get finance. It must be looked at during the year. If the author of the Plan reports back to me with changes during the year, I regard that as a positive feature.

'The Plan must build in sensitivities. The Plan says "This is what we think will happen". It sets out the number of widgets sold, the suppliers' price and who the customers are. But the Plan should also address the worst case. If sales drop by 20%, interest rises by 3% and debtors take longer to pay than expected, for example. But the sensitivity analysis must not become too detailed. The point of the analysis is to show the company will still be able to operate if conditions move against it. It is often not appreciated that the reverse can also cause problems – what if sales grow by 20%, how will that affect cash flow? Will working capital requirements increase?

'To me, it is a fundamental part of planning that companies review Plans regularly. To be aware that market trends are changing before sales drop dramatically, can be the difference between success and failure. Using the route map analogy, they can often see the traffic hold up and change direction before it is too late.

'The qualitative and quantitative aspects of the Plan are both important. I need to see the guts of the Plan in the document presented to me. If the person really under-stands what the company is doing, the numbers are likely to be more accurate. Anyone can put together the numbers to satisfy a banker. But the banker needs to look behind the scenes to see if the numbers are likely to make sense – and make sure words and figures do not differ!

'Non-financial aspects are very important to me. And in addition to looking at the people, their experience, succession, etc., I have a check list to catch obvious things in a Plan, which may not have been thought about. My PESTEL list. The P is for Political. Is there any political influence which may affect the business? A betting company, for example, may be very affected if the government changes its attitude towards betting. The E stands for Environmental considerations. Is there any government legislation which requires more expensive processing than allowed for in the Plan? Green issues are, of course, very topical. Or are there any changes which will require heavy capital expenditure shortly?

'The Sociological aspects of a Plan cover such things as current fashions. A furrier's Plan a few years ago would have been wholly unrealistic if it omitted to reduce its turnover without any diversification. Next is Technological. Is the company affected by technological development? A company making record players would have to have developed into the CD market if it wanted to continue its expansion. The Economic considerations come next. These have a particular relevance during a recession. Finally, the Legal point. Is the company operating within the law? Is planning consent needed for a new property, for example?

'People who think they have drawn up the best Plans have sometimes drawn up the worst. If the Plan looks pukka, presented neatly, etc., it is still so easy to skip over the fundamentals. I find people generally don't have enough training or reference material to put together good Business Plans. A good accountant should be brought in early on. There is almost never consideration of what the company will do, for example, if prices are forced to drop by 10% or if debtors take one month longer to pay than expected. Most entrepreneurs, but clearly not all, are so enthusiastic about their own business that they appear to wear blinkers when downside factors are highlighted.

'I would estimate that of the Plans I see, 25% are excellent, 25% are good or adequate, with the remainder ranging from barely adequate to very poor.

'If a company is small, it is able to run without massive validation or collation of data. This is because the management will have a fairly good idea from their direct knowledge of events. But as a company grows, management become divorced from some of the more routine areas of the business. There comes a stage in every company's development where it becomes critical that a Plan is put in place to give back to management that overview they used to have. The majority of companies grow well beyond that stage before they realize the problem. I think we would all agree that memories are often found wanting and it is important to put things down on paper – how many of us thought during the week of the odd jobs to do at the weekend at home, only to forget them until Monday morning!

'In my view, one of the most critical of all factors of a Business Plan is that management must avoid kidding themselves that the business is better than it is – the only people you are going to fool is yourself.'

Mark Wickham – UCB Bank

Mark Wickham is a Corporate Loan Executive of the UCB Luton Bank branch. The majority of his business dealings have been in the Northern Home Counties. The

bank has an aggressive policy towards growth, despite the recession. This requires the managers to have a clear understanding of risks involved with a loan. The borrower must have good security to back high-risk loans.

'I hate waffle. It turns me off completely. I want to be interested when looking at a Plan. So brochures and photographs catch my attention. I also want to know as soon as possible what the company's requirements are – how much does the company want to borrow or what size facilities are required, to get an overview of what the deal is.

'Then lead on to prove to me how the business works and how the loan will satisfy its requirements. They need to show that the management know what they are doing, that I will be happy with their experience. I also want to see that the company can service the loan and that the bank will be secure.

'I recently saw a good Plan. It immediately outlined its requirements. They said why the bank should lend, how they would pay back the bank and what security was available to protect the loan. They set out the experience of management. This was all on the first page. On the front of the document was a photograph of the product and on the back were details. The next thirty pages were confirmation of the first page.

'It is difficult to know how influenced I am by the first page. I think I make my mind up within the first five minutes of looking at a Plan. Because if the company is able to convey precisely and accurately the points it is trying to make, it is likely to have good salesmen – they should be able to portray to their customers these ideas, which is key to the success of the business. If it is able to do so quickly with the bank, it is likely to be able to do so with its clients. I perceive the Plan to be a document which sells the company to the bank.

'If the Plan is well organized, it indicates the management will be well organized. They need to have financial controls, management controls and personnel skills. If controls exist, the organization is likely to be able to grow. Many banks will not wish to lend to a business whose growth will remain static within the next three to ten years.

'My main criticism of Plans is that they tend to contain irrelevant information. Of the Plans I see, I would rank less than 10% as being good, more than 30% as being bad and the rest as indifferent. By bad, I mean that the style is bad, as distinct from the content of the Plan. Some Plans which would be acceptable are rejected if badly set out. If there is a marginal deal and the people seem committed to the company, a good Business Plan will swing the deal.

'I believe there are three basic criteria banks have for lending. Firstly, do the applicants know what they are doing? Secondly, is there sufficient security to back the proposal? Thirdly, is the loan serviceable – will the applicant be able to repay the interest as well as the capital when due? The security aspect is the key distinction between the requirements of a bank and a venture capitalist.

'The bank wants to know the people involved – the past successes, background, etc. It is assumed they do not have the experience if they do not say so. About 85% of Business Plans I look at come from new customers. If there is a lack of experience, that does not automatically kill things. I was looking at a proposal to finance acquiring a nursing home recently. It was a positive thing to see that the management did not have adequate experience, because they were acknowledging their shortfall – we can ensure experience is recruited before advancing the loan. I have more respect for a person who can see a problem from the bank's point of view.

'I do not need to see a market analysis. I am indifferent if it is there or not. I do not like to see too much detail. I want an appreciation of the market rather than an in-depth analysis.

'The main causes of failure I have seen recently are key personnel leaving and market failure. I have seen many businesses run worse than they could have been run for lack of financial controls. These are the main reasons for failure. When I am looking at a Business Plan, these are some of the key factors that I am looking to be reassured about. All I have to look at is what is in the document. This is why a good Plan has a strong sway on the end result of whether a loan will be finally advanced.'

John Greig – FennoScandia Bank

FennoScandia is a small commercial bank. It is the UK subsidiary of a larger Finnish bank. Part of its business is carried out with Finnish customers on behalf of its parent bank. Part of its function is to act in an independent capacity within the UK market.

The bank has a small team of dynamic, young, capable managers who are able to respond quickly and efficiently to banking proposals. John Greig is one of the team managers with a particular responsibility for business with turnover ranging from around £2 million to £30 million, although he has been involved in considering proposals outside this range.

'Many people regard Business Plans as a number exercise. The greatest challenge is to create documentation from which you are able to quantify the non-financial parts of the business – and to make them explicit. This means setting out clearly the assumptions underlying the Plan and describing the environment in which the business is placed. Typically, business with less than £20 million turnover does not dominate the market unless it is in a niche area.

'Generally, from the Plans I have seen, they tend not to go into the market structure. They often fail to give a clear picture of competitors and competitive advantage they may have. The main reason that this part is needed in a Plan is to allow evaluation of how likely the turnover forecast is to succeed. If a small company Plans an increase in market share of, say, 5%, in a market that is dominated by a large corporation, you would have to question whether the larger company will tolerate this loss of business. They may have decided to leave the gap in the market that the small company is filling, because it does not suit their overhead structure or production facilities to operate in that area. But that does not mean they will allow the company to move into their part of the market.

'I think I have never seen a Plan which does not predict growth. Often, growth does not come in the first year or two – the company may even project losses. I can understand that a shareholder may not desire to put money into a business to support losses. Equally, the banker has little interest in funding losses and would only be prepared to do so if the shareholders take the major part of the risk, and if profits can be generated within a reasonable time scale. However, where the banking criteria are met, growth is certainly not a prerequisite for lending. In a few circumstances, excess growth is a barrier to lending.

'It is important that the planner is aware of the purpose of preparing a Business Plan.

The primary purpose of a Business Plan should be for the company itself. It is a very important aspect of running a business. If a Plan is produced only occasionally, for the financiers, it questions the Plan's validity. A company with a £20 million turnover, for example, must produce regular budgets and forecasts these days, if it wants to succeed. It is the only way to cope with the rapid change in the business cycle of changing interest rates, exchange rates and demand. It has to produce a cash flow, profits and balance sheet forecast.

'It is especially important when looking at a business's strategy. The point is to avoid having to react to circumstances once they have hit the business. The company should look at the portfolio of its products. It should look at what customers might want to buy from you. The company must look at the trends of the market. Planning helps clarify the effect and consequences of the trends.

A major criteria for bank lending must be positive cash flows. It is as much as the security of the underlying assets. There is another category that the banks may want to lend to. That is where the company has been hit by circumstances that the business could not have predicted, but management have reacted well and successfully dealt with the problem to find a solution.

'Forecasts are little more than an attempt to predict the future. Their main value is to provide a benchmark to compare actual results with. If the Plan shows a particular cash requirement in several months time and the actual results were worse in the first two months, you can know with virtual certainty that the cash requirements are going to be higher than expected. Either action must be taken to compensate for the shortfall or the bank must be contacted immediately. There is nothing worse than being told for the first time of a problem, a week before money is due to run out.

'Management should be realistic when forecasting. If a company has a long lead time requirement to add to the order book, it must work around known business, at least until there is a possibility that the new business generated will hit the company's turnover.

'Most banks' criteria for lending money will be tightening up in future. The banks were able to rely on spiralling property and other asset values to back lending during the last boom. It was the banks that mainly provided liquidity to the market that caused the dramatic rise in asset values. However, with so many companies failing to repay interest or capital, many UK banks face sizeable loan losses. Now that property prices are falling and company's balance sheets are shrinking, companies need to reflect the assumption that funding may not be as available in the future. This will become a critical part of future planning. Trading must be strong enough not just to pay the interest but also to sustain repaying capital. If a company has strong growth, it must have good margins to produce sufficient profits to find at least part of the increased working capital needs at that level of activity.

'I believe banking should be virtually risk free. With loans attracting a 1.5% to 3% margin, from which all overheads must be paid, there is little room for bad debts. We are looking for high margins, good profit cover for interest and asset cover for the capital, a profitable business and low gearing. If more funding is needed than that, the company should be looking to increase its equity base. When considering the risk, trading risk also needs to be considered. How dependent is the company on restricted suppliers or customers? How dependent is the success of the company on competition?

'The clearing banks will face increased pressure on margins. They will have to increase them. They are forced to make the profitable business pay for the failures. This is where smaller commercial banks may be most suitable for companies. Where they are essentially strong banking propositions, but the clearing banks are unable to see the strength or to offer a sufficiently competitive service.

'I am a lot more concerned about where business is introduced from than the Business Plan, initially. There is a lack of time to be able to look at all deals we are presented. But that does not mean the document is not very important. If the Plan is badly produced, with wrong information, without proper explanations of assumptions or not detailed enough over the next eighteen months or so, I am unable to evaluate the proposal. The Plan should have past results with very up-to-date management accounts. If they are not available, management are not keeping close enough control on the business.

'One of the things I like to look at is the summary in the first part. I like to see in summary what the business is about, what are its needs and why the funds are needed. I was once told by a past boss of mine that if I had read all the Plan at the first meeting, I would probably be the only one in the room to have done so.

'There is one final point. It is extremely important to understand the background of the people involved. At the end of the day, it is the management who get it right or wrong. I am looking for their experience and competence. It is not possible to tell from the Plan all you need to know about management, but it sets the scene.

'Banking is going back to its basics. Funding will be more difficult to arrange. The planning process is becoming a most important tool to deal with this extra difficulty that management must contend with.'

Dan Nash – Merchant Banker

Dan Nash set up and managed Citibank's European Trading Company (CITC) before moving to Mitsubishi and Singer & Friedlander with responsibility for their Special Projects departments. He is now the Managing Director of Excell International Limited, a trading company which negotiates and organizes special commodity transactions around the world.

'Judging business propositions is different from running a business in which you are experienced. As such, you need better precedents to draw on to be able to judge whether, for example, a business will be able to save on labour or increase efficiency. A venture capitalist will not know whether the proposition is impossible and must look between the lines. You will be looking at the business for organization, integrity, ability, experience.

'I invested in a database company called "MAID". The company provides a mass information base on almost any industry you can think of. It collates an incredible number of publications on computer for easy retrieval by thousands of users. Its running costs are frightening. The Managing Director convinced me that by year two, £1 million would be made. As a capitalist, I discounted it and thought it could happen by year 3. Here we are at year 5, and we are still not making £1 million, although we are close. To look at propositions, you need to inject realism into forecasts. Spreadsheets and other "gismos" are useful as a gauge, but limited in use. You must ensure you are aware it is a gamble, unless it is a proven business.

'You are looking for a compelling rationale. In practice, all figures should be discounted. Look in detail at the market position. For example, is the demand there for the product or services? This is the economic rationale. And is there an existing supply to meet that demand? That is it! Figures can only be a "guesstimate'. Therefore the whole evaluation is, Does the proposal make sense? If it does, then put meat on the bones.

'If you ask me what should be in a Plan, I say to you I don't understand your business. Put it down in writing to explain it to me. I am a man with money. Prove to me you will use the money well. Much information comes from thin air. If you are trying to convince me, it must be based on reality. If you have a new invention, that reality will be impossible to provide. You must show me convincing, bona fide projections – and then I say to you, it's all a guessing game anyway.'

17 Lawyers

A Business Plan is an enticement to someone to lend to or buy a business. John Hargreaves of Franks Charlesly & Co, a firm of City solicitors, is frequently asked to advise investors and bankers who believe they have been misled. He is expert at picking holes in arguments put before him. His comments are not a comprehensive legal dissertation on Business Plans. The subject would be a book in itself. But his views are nonetheless sobering.

'One of the greatest misnomers of the law is the warning "*caveat emptor*" – let the buyer (the banker or investor) beware. It means that it is the responsibility of the buyer to make sure what is being bought is what is expected. In truth, if your Business Plan is to be used to persuade a bank or an investor – or an outright purchaser for that matter – the saying should be "let the representor beware".

'Whether in a bank's credit agreement or buried in the thick of an investment or sale agreement, you can expect information warranties. If the document contains a statement such as:

> All information provided . . . in connection with this Agreement . . . was true, complete and accurate [or] the Directors are not aware of any material facts or circumstances not disclosed . . .,

you are in the realm of express contractual warranties. What do they mean?

'If any of the information turns out to have been inaccurate, you may be held liable to make good the loss suffered through your misrepresentation. If you say that creditors are £1.5 million when they are, in fact, £1.7 million, you could find a bill for £200,000 in the post. If you say the profits of the business will be £250,000 and they turn out to be £50,000, you may find a bill of not just £200,000 for the lost profit, but a lot more for the lost value of potential investment. It is comforting to note that this type of legal action rarely goes undefended and in any event it is worth noting some of the areas where legal and accounting advice can help you.

'Let me explain some points in relation to written terms or agreements first. The information warranties I mention above, like the examples, lack certainty, for what

100

exactly have you informed the other side and what exactly is being relied on? "All information . . ." will include any information given both in writing and verbally and over an indefinite period. The first rule, therefore, is "be precise" and press for your opposite number to agree what you are and are not supposed to be underwriting. It is always best to agree to a written list, but only advance as representations, statements which you have verified.

'The way you represent or warrant information as being factual depends on the information concerned. Historic accounting information, by its nature, is rarely complete, but it should be "fair" and "reasonable". Forecasts, the meat of the Plan, are not strictly "true" or "accurate" but they should be prepared on reasonable assumptions and represent your honest and reasonable belief.

'Sometimes these representations are intended to have a continuing effect by the investor or banker. The information given is correct when given and is intended to remain correct throughout the life of the agreement. Examples include a bank's requirement that debtors do not fall below a minimum level compared with the bank's loans and overdrafts, and an investor's requirement that there are presently no unprofitable contracts and there will be none taken on during the life of his investment. Although you may feel able to verify these facts at the outset, the situation may change. And if they may, you need wording to deal with this.

'A more balanced information warranty might then read:

To the best of A's knowledge and belief the written information appearing in the Business Plan appended to this Agreement and initialled for identification is at the date of this Agreement and in all material respects true and fair in respect of historic accountings information and true and accurate in respect of other historic information . . . [and if appropriate add] . . . and will remain so on each date upon which this representation is repeated for the purposes of this Agreement save as to the extent that A makes written disclosure to B on or before that time.

'The projections in the Business Plan attached to this Agreement and initialled for the purpose of identification, have been prepared by A in good faith and on fair and reasonable assumptions, and subject to such assumptions represent A's honest and reasonable belief as to the subject matter of the same. B confirms that he has relied solely on the Business Plan in entering into this Agreement and upon no other representation of A.'

'Note that there are several phrases designed to protect you. The final paragraph is intended to make clear the information relied on and I refer further to this below. You are also permitted to disclose against future repetitions of the statement which can really nullify its effect. The reference to your state of knowledge is important, but having said this Directors will be expected to be apprised of the affairs of their company. Note also the reference to materiality. When partners' trading relations start to turn sour, litigation on relatively minor matters is something to avoid. With this type of clause you would be more in control of the position. But you would be responsible if, as has happened in America, you wrote about sales of life assurance policies which would have required sales to five times more people than live in the whole world, each year! Whether dealing with a bank or investor, your projections will be an important factor in their decision to trade with you. Views as to what are or are not "reasonable" assumptions for any projection differ widely and it can only help to agree these with your accountants and lay the assumptions out on the face of the Plan.

'No agreement will cover every conceivable situation and hence so much litigation arises out of what are thought of as "watertight" agreements. However, even without an express information warranty in your document, legislation can come to the aid of the banker of investor, if it or he feels he has been induced by misstatement to proceed with you. The Misrepresentation Act of 1967 provides that if a representation is made which induces a third party to enter into a contract, and that representation proves false, the contract can in certain circumstances, be overturned. Thus the absence of that form of working should never be seen as a licence to mislead which can in itself be fraud. Indeed if a sale of shares or other securities is involved, the law imposes further teeth by imposing criminal liability on the dishonest in certain circumstances – as some famous names in the past will attest – as well as requiring a formal prospectus in certain circumstances.

'It is also common in Business Plans to incorporate a paragraph stating what is fact and what conjecture and this can help your position if there could possibly be doubt on the point. Distinguishing between audited and unaudited information is worthwhile. Setting out the source of any information in the Plan will help. Incorporating on the face of the Plan a clause adapted from the 'representations' example earlier in the chapter may also be beneficial.

'When dealing with banks, the terms tend to be more specific and comprehensive. Assume you have negotiated at great length and with great care a term from your bankers. On the basis of knowing that funds exist to allow specific developments, you spend money or commit funds over the term of the loan. If the loan is called in early it could be disastrous and you want to guard against this.

'If the loan is from a clearing bank, generally, they give only informal comfort that they will not call in the loan within the term of the loan, and more usually state that the facilities can be called up "on demand". A typical clause might read:

> Whilst it is not our intention presently to require payment within 5 years, we reserve the right to make immediate demand . . .

'Other lenders may have given a stronger commitment about repayment dates but subject to a right to accelerate repayment in the event of there being an "event of default" (usually defined in the Agreement). The problem is that "an event of default" may occur even to the strongest of companies and could happen quite inadvertently. The definition of "event of default" may not necessarily be connected with a breach by you of the terms of the loan or be fault-based, and could relate perhaps to your breach of a quite separate agreement. The so-called cross default provision, which can be particularly concerning where you have a number of term loans, which can all fall in together through a default on just one – the "house of cards" effect.

'The key to preserving your loan is to consider carefully the loan agreement's provisions before you commit to them and to negotiate, as far as possible, sensible events of default: that is, events that give your bank adequate protection but allow you to operate sensibly without defaulting, at best (from your standpoint), to limit the calling in of a loan to situations where the consequence of the breaches has such an effect as will prevent you from properly attending to your obligations under the loan documents. Also look for a "breathing space" period to put things right between being notified by the bank that a default has occurred and the time the loan can be recalled.

'Assuming you have done everything possible to produce certainty and you have been advised that all assumptions are reasonable, are there any further protections?

'There are a variety of limitation clauses far more common for investors' contracts than banking agreements. They tend to fall into three main categories. The first is time-based. The investor confirms that they are only entitled to bring action, if relevant, within say five years for a taxation claim and a shorter period for other claims. The second is value-based. Action can only be brought if the claim exceeds say 5% of the received price (to avoid trifling claims) and there is an upper aggregate limit equal to the total value you have obtained. Another useful protection is shown in the final paragraph of our example and is what is termed by lawyers as "sole reliance" provisions. The investor will make an express statement that he has relied only on certain information and not on anything further in deciding to enter into the contract. This is useful to focus attention on what is believed to be the key issues since it is easier for you to know which information needs to be verified.'

When discussing this section with John Hargreaves, he went to great lengths to impress that there are many other aspects of law that may be relevant to any specific Business Plan and that no action should be taken without the benefit of your own legal and accounting advice. He was trying to place the Plan in some form of legal context where it is to be used to persuade a third party to part with money for the benefit of you or your company. He stressed the value of interaction between the lawyers and accountants for your protection, and that the earlier advice is taken, the better. Despite the common belief within the commercial world about whose responsibility it is to ensure money is invested or lent wisely, he is adamant, 'let the representor beware'.

18　Accountants

Jonathan Cohen is a founder partner of Vandenburghs, Chartered Accountants. He was also a financial director of a property investment company and is currently a director of a financial management company. As a partner in Vandenburghs, he is responsible for preparing Plans for clients in management, focusing their Plans for running their business at banks and at investors ranging from venture capitalists to joint venture trading partners. He is also involved in evaluation of Plans prepared by companies his clients are looking to invest in or lend to.

This chapter sets out how an accountant sees the requirements of preparing a Business Plan and what to include in it. It is aimed at producing a document which the management, as investors of the company's shareholders' funds, requires.

Introduction

'A Business Plan is prepared to help management and the investor to assess what the plans of the business are and how likely those plans will be achieved. After you have devised your Plan, you will need to make the same assessment as the investor and the banker to ensure that your Plans can be achieved.

'There is no standard format for a Plan except that it is a document that, by its nature, will be read by other people and, most probably, at a time when you are not there to explain it to them.

'The Business Plan is also an internal document and will be used by managers to follow the direction which has been planned by the board. Too much hype will confuse the managers as they will be led by the higher expectations in the Plan.

'The Business Plan has a separate chapter for selected information required to evaluate the Plan. In some cases, you might want to run some sections together. For instance, the management and corporate structure sections can be integrated with the section on explanation of the business. Once you have established who will read the Plan you can cut your cloth accordingly, but remember to highlight the information your reader is likely to want to know.

Explanation of the Business

Nature of the trade

'In order to help the investor assess whether the business is capable of achieving its target, it is necessary to explain the trade of the business. This will also help the investor to decide whether he wants to deal with this company in the first place. You will often hear bankers decline proposals because they claim that they do not understand the business they have been asked to invest in. This section is your bid to make them understand.

'Businesses are often divided into various companies or divisions depending on the different types of trade carried out. Your business might only have one trading centre. Each separate activity should be described separately. You will not need to go into great detail. For instance, you will not need to explain detailed scientific processes but you should explain that there is the process. You should also describe the marketplace in which you are operating. If the marketplace is well known, there is no need to go into detail. For instance, you might say that "Division A is a machine tool manufacturer working for the capital equipment industry"; or you might say that "Division B provides design services to Defence Industry in the Home Counties as one of the largest of only three specialist companies servicing an annual spend of £30 million.'

'Once you have divided up your business, use this as a base for the rest of the document. You should then show the relative size of each division within the organization; the number of employees, the profits or losses of that division, the location and the proportion of the overall funding of that division. To make the report more readable, this summary can be in tabular form:

Division	Trade	Profits/ (Losses) (£)	Employees	Funds (£)	Location
A	Machine tools	100,000	38	500,000	Hull
B	Design	(10,000)	7	40,000	London
C	Equipment sales	40,000	15	80,000	Crawley
		130,00	60	620,000	

Market strength

'The investor will want to assess to what extent achievement of your targets is dependent upon factors outside your control. For instance, you will not be able to expand your business beyond the size of the marketplace, so the Plan should show your position in the marketplace.

'You should also show for example:

1   Your main customers and their importance to the business.
2   Your mains suppliers and their importance to the business.
3   Any scarce resources which might affect the business.
4   Strength of the competition.
5   Likely changes in the marketplace.

Financial structure of the company

'The investor and the manager will need to decide how the business should be financed. Of course, he will need to understand the present financing arrangements.

'Financial structuring varies between companies. Simple arrangements might be described as "A working capital requirement of £120,000, financed in part by the reserves of the company and in part by an overdraft facility of £100,000. The average balance of the overdraft is £75,000 and all outstanding amounts are secured by a personal guarantee of the directors and a charge on the home of Mr X, the Chairman."

Strengths of the business

'The investor will also have to assess what factors within the business will affect its ability to meet targets. The Business Plan should show what are the strengths of the company – for example the management, highly specialized skills, access to cheap supplies, good relations with customers or an exclusive licence. Of course, you should show how you intend to maintain the strengths in the future. For all those natural salesmen in management, this is your opportunity to shine, but don't go overboard.

Weaknesses of the business

'You should also "confess" to your weaknesses. There is no harm in this – every business has weaknesses and they cannot be avoided. In fact, recognizing weaknesses is the first sign of good housekeeping. If you cannot find anything wrong with your business at all, then you won't be looking for outside finance in the first place.

'Given that you cannot avoid some weaknesses, the second sign of good housekeeping is laying plans to reduce the effects of those weaknesses. For example, if you are too reliant on one customer, you should try to look to spread your turnover or at least try to ensure that your customer will stay with you for as long as you will be reliant on his business. Alternatively, you might want to acquire stocks of rare materials so that you can reduce your reliance on third parties in times of high consumption.

'Your investor will want to assess the financial effects of the measures you take. To maintain customer loyalty you might have to give a discount; stock holding can involve substantial costs. Your plans will measure to what extent it is worth avoiding your weaknesses and the investor will want to assess this.

Overall strategy

'The Business Plan shows what your business will achieve in a limited time period and how you plan to do so. This forms part of your overall strategy for the long term. For example, your longer-term plans might include domination of your current marketplace; you might want to diversify by expanding the present market or changing into different trades. Your Business Plan should show what your longer-term aims are and how this plan fits into your aims. This will help the investor assess whether management is committed to the plan and the likely direction of the company after the period of the plan. This section need not be too long. For example:

> Our aim is to increase the company's market share to 20% within five years to enable us to enjoy the additional profits that go with economies that can be made with a larger company. Growth by additional investment is estimated to increase our turnover to £5m. in the next financial year which will bring our market share to 18%.

Long tomes planning world domination tend to become confusing and, given the length of time in the future being forecast, tend to be unreliable.

Management and Corporate Structure

'Whether or not you are planning world domination, businesses have a habit of growing by addition of subsidiaries and divisions. Any budding Napoleon will help to build his empire with the creation of his own management structure. The sales manager will employ a deputy sales manager who, in turn, will employ the assistant deputy sales manager and so on.

'An investor can lose sight of the real trades of the business with all the different companies and people within them pulling in apparently different directions. Your business plan would be more readable if it contains a chart of where all the companies fit into the group and a separate chart of management and their responsibilities. To keep things simple, the company chart should include only parts of the business which provide a significant part of the overall activity – for example, dormant companies can be excluded. The management chart should represent only key personnel.

'With most small businesses, the management tends to comprise the owners of the business. At this point, you might include a note about each of the principal managers/ owners. This is to help the investor assess who is running the company and what will happen to the profits made if the plans come to fruition. To avoid clogging up this section with details of academic and technical merit, you can include CVs of the principals in an appendix at the end of the plan. If your business is very large, you might want to add a bit of explanation about management roles.

'The investor will almost certainly lend great weight to the skills, cohesion and experience of management. The Business Plan provides incentive to management to ensure that the right person is doing the right job.

Plans for the Period Covered by the Document

'A Business Plan represents the detail of the tactics that will be employed over a relatively short term – usually one to three years. This is the mechanism by which the business will achieve its aims.

'So far, your business plan will have included details of the background against which the plan will be put into operation. This section of the document will include the nuts and bolts of what will have to be done to make the plan work. This section will cause you the most difficulty in terms of preparation. You should be clear in your own mind what plans you have for increased profitability and investments. If you manage the business, you probably understand it more than anyone else. With advice, you are better placed to see the way forward, the openings in the market and the potential for profit. This section should set out your ideas for others to understand.

'You will have to include some technical explanation of the tasks ahead. But take extra special care not to confuse your reader with jargon. You are trying to persuade an investor that his money will go to achieving certain targets which will produce a return for him and the business. If he cannot understand what the plans are, he will not be able to assess the likelihood of success. You will need to keep the attention of the investor – who understands less about your product than you.

'In order to keep a structure to this section, concentrate your efforts on three areas:

1   How you will exploit your strengths and what action you propose to take to realize and invest profits.
2   How you will reduce the effects of your weaknesses and what action you will take to prevent losses.
3   Other areas you will move into to develop the trade in terms of profit generation and investment.

'Keep to short, punchy paragraphs such as:

1a   We propose to increase our market share to 20% and for that purpose it will be necessary to acquire a new production machine which will be faster and more reliable than the present system. The new machine will allow for night work if necessary.
A new factory will not be required to house this new machine but it is anticipated that a second machine will be required in two years' time, at which point alternative accommodation will be sought.

1b   We propose to place an order for one ton of copper per month at a fixed rate to avoid the difficulties that arise with fulfilling forward order with a fluctuating product price.

1c   We propose to move John Smith from the production team to head the buying department, to avoid confusion about what materials best suit the production line. John's deputy Ron Jones will take over as production manager.

1d   We will continue to invest 3% of turnover into research and development to ensure that we stay ahead of the field in new products.

It might be helpful if the paragraphs are numbered as they will be referred to throughout the document.

'Try to avoid any technical information in this part of the report. You can always produce technical results in an appendix. For example, you might say:

We propose to buy a new machine which will decrease our labour requirement by 12% and increase our productivity by 24% in a full year. Our eventual aim is to mechanize to the extent that all skilled labour requirements are replaced by computer controllers.'

This is not to say that an investor would not want to investigate the accuracy of your statement. You will have to have the facts and figures at your disposal – but not in the Plan to overwhelm the investor. This is the quickest way to a big turn-off.

Financial Effects of the Plan

'Finance is very much behind your plan. The Business Plan forms part of your financial planning. Bringing in outside investors is only one part of that Plan. Your business has its own cash resources which need husbanding. Even if you are not looking for funds from outside the business, you still need to allocate your own cash.

'Your business runs to make money and you need money from investors to make new investments yourself. It follows that the investor's prime concern will be to see that you are making enough money out of your plans to provide him with a return on his money, and to pay him back eventually and ensure that you are getting enough out of all this to keep you happy working for the business.

'The financial effects of the plans will relate to the specific task undertaken as well as the overall change to the business. The Plan should tie up the specific plans as shown in the previous section with the financial effects and any technical details shown in the appendices. For this, you might find it helpful to follow the same paragraph numeration as shown in the previous section. For example:

> The new machinery would cost £100,000 to buy and install and would provide an increased turnover of £80,000. Because the labour requirements of the machinery are lower and because the machinery can be used at night if required, the increased contribution to profits would be £20,000 in the first year and £35,000 in subsequent years at today's values. The increases in turnover are not certain, in particular during the period of recession.

This is sufficient information to enable the investor to assess the value of the investment against its cost. Your financial projections will show the overall cash and profit flows. In this section you can cut the meat on the bones of those projections by showing how the overall package is made up. For example, your cash flow will show the effects of all the investments. It will show the aggregate funding required and the overall changes on profitability. This section can explain the component parts of the picture.

Funding Proposals and Requirements

'The presentation of a business plan to an investor is similar to the presentation of a deal to a merchant banker. Up until now, you will have been describing your part of the bargain. You show what you will do to justify the resources he will be providing. This section will show what the investor is to get out of the deal.

'When you are preparing a business plan internally without the need to raise cash externally, you are carrying out a similar process. You need to ensure that your own resources which you are allocating are being spent on the best investment available to you.

'Quite often, the investor will work out his own deal as a condition for investing. At worst, this section will provide the investor with the information he requires to make up his own mind; at best you can point the investor in the direction you want to go. The investor needs to know the following:

1   Are the funds invested going to provide a return both to pay him and make enough for you?
2   What kind of investment do you need and how long will the payback period be?
3   What are the risks that investor will not get his money back and how can those risks be reduced?
4   If things go wrong, how can the investor ensure that he will get his money back anyway?

'The investor will be assessing the likelihood of a profit on the basis of the information you have already provided in the plan. He will assess the feasibility of the project, the capability of the managers and the strength of the market. The investor will also examine whether the return you have shown is possible. An investor will not want the project to make enough money simply to cover the interest on his investment. He will want the project to show a profit for the managers as well, so that they have the incentive to carry out the task. Often, the investor will want the amount of profit earned by the company before interest charges to be twice the interest charged. This ratio is known as interest cover.

'The investor will also look at the effects of the investment on the business. A business must remain reasonably liquid so that it can pay its debts as they fall due. If the investment absorbs too much cash, it will not be able to pay its debts. The strength of the balance sheet depends on its liquidity and the relationship between its assets and liabilities, often known as gearing. Much is said about the ideal level of gearing and this will depend on the industry you are in.

'Whilst money will always remain money, it often comes in different shades of the same colour. Banks will have depositors who wish to leave their money for different periods. Similarly, your investments might require different periods of funding. When you buy a new machine, it might take some time for the machine to turn in a profit. It could take several years before enough profit is earned to repay the loan acquired to buy it. If the payback period is five years, you will require finance for a five-year term. Conversely, if you are borrowing to fund working capital requirements, you will need funds that are flexible to reflect the constant variations in working capital.

'By and large, the investor will come up with his own ideas of the type of loans he will make. It might help your arguments if you place down a marker as to what kind of finance you will need.

'The investor will assess his own risk. You cannot second-guess all that risk but where you can assess his risk, you can put his mind at ease by showing what you are doing to reduce the exposure. For example, an investor might be lending money to carry out an order for your customer. Without that order being placed, the investor would avoid making his investment. This becomes a difficulty where an investor has already provided funds for your business. You would prefer not to repay any loans, whilst the investor would prefer not to continue his investment whilst at risk. Your plan should show what steps you are taking to reduce the investor's (and your own) risks.

'Almost all investors – and always the banks – want to know that if things go wrong, they will get their money back. The only way to do this is to lend against certain assets. Quite often, assets are acquired with funds from the investor. It follows that these funds will be secured against the assets bought. This is always the case when you acquire assets on hire purchase or by finance lease.

'Investors will certainly need to know what assets are available to be used as security. If you have your own ideas as to what assets might be available for security, it would help if you say so here. For example, one Director might be prepared to put up his home as security whilst his co-Director might not. If your factory is already mortgaged, now's the time to speak up.

Other Matters

'There are often non-financial matters which would have an effect on the investment plans. For example, the Articles of the company might restrict the borrowing powers of the Directors. Whilst the proposed investment might be within the current limits, a second investment might take the company over the limit. If your local authority is planning a motorway where your factory now stands, it might be helpful to volunteer the information now.

Appendices: Financial Information, Technical Data and CVs

'The appendices will not form the main body of the report because they tend to be quantitative rather than qualitative. The amount of information you provide will depend on the amount your investor will already have. The last set of audited accounts represents the last certain market, but it would also be helpful to provide any management accounts with an up-to-date balance sheet. You should provide projections as to how you see the profits and cash-flow over the period of the Plan after taking into account all your proposals. You might also want to produce a projected balance sheet at certain points over that period. You cannot hope to project accurately for more than about a year and any projections beyond then will include a certain amount of guesswork.

'You will have put your technical data in an appendix so that it will not clog up the commercial and financial value of the report. Anything you provide here should be of sufficient depth so that the investor can understand the processes you operate. The problem lies in that the investor will not understand your business as well as you. You must explain the process to him but in terms that he can understand. The technical detail should not include reams of third-party information which the investor can collect for himself. If the investor cannot understand your business at all, you should consider how appropriate the investor is for your business.

'The CVs can be included to identify the strengths and weaknesses of the managers. The CV is not there to glorify the Chairman or to justify the purchase of his second Rolls-Royce. Such a Chairman can normally justify his own Rolls-Royce without the need for a business plan. The CV can cover only a page of text with an inclusion of the following:

1 Personal details such as age, marital status, family, etc.
2 Any qualifications earned.
3 Job experience; but this should be limited to the employer's name, job title, period of employment and a description of the work. You don't need to go back to Adam and Eve for your job history, just go back enough to fill up your page.

'The final document will include a summary of your plans for a certain period in the future; it will include details of how much your plans will cost and how much you will get back from those plans. Your Plan will show how you propose to fund your plans and whether the return justifies the funding.

'Your Business Plan is not a sales document for your products, but it represents your plans – so it must make sense to you. Nevertheless, you will want your investor to read it and enjoy it. Try not to make the Plan too long; about twenty pages should be the maximum but five or ten pages will often do the trick. Your Plan should be capable of making sense to your colleagues and any investor; and it must be capable of being monitored throughout the period of the Plan.'

Part 6

Examples

19   Background to Business Plans

It is often difficult to visualize how a Business Plan can work best for your business. Two real Business Plans are set out in this section of the book. They are based on genuine businesses with typical opportunities and problems. Some of the background of each of the organizations is set out below. For reasons of confidentiality, some of the details have been changed or omitted.

This chapter outlines some of the considerations which are not set out in the Plans. Many decisions are made prior to finalizing the Plan. Some of these are touched upon below. They illustrate part of the planning process which takes place before the Plan is committed to paper.

The City University Business School: Management Development Centre

The Centre is one of three segments of the City University Business School. The activities of the Centre are stated clearly in the Plan. It is a training organization for business. Over the last few years, the Centre has become increasingly profit-motivated and has developed independent reporting facilities for control.

The Plan was devised towards the beginning of the entry to the 1989–92 recession. Some of the Centre's bookings were beginning to be delayed or cancelled. The Gulf War at the start of 1991 had had a direct impact on attendances for two reasons: International delegates were travelling abroad less and the Centre has a small operation in the Gulf. The operation was severely affected by the shaken confidence of business in the Middle East. In the UK, some of the Centre's regular clients had delayed courses that had been booked. Many of the courses aimed at the general public of the business world saw declining attendances. But the Centre had been working hard at developing new courses with partial success. Some important new businesses were added to the clientele. The net result was that turnover was holding up – but only just.

The Centre's plan for last year had been to expand. This year, when the sensitivity planning had been evaluated, it was concluded that the risk of turnover reducing below earlier targets was sufficiently high to warrant a slowdown in the growth plans. They would be delayed for a couple of years to allow the effects of recession to rage and die down.

The Centre is part of the City University. Increasingly, the school is viewed as a commercial enterprise with a clear profit objective. How this will affect the Centre is difficult to forecast. In practical terms, it is expected that there will not be a significant change in how the Centre will be run over the next couple of years. At present, the Centre is managed reasonably autonomously. The pressure on profits will have little impact on the expected trends of the market in future. Therefore, a fundamental issue to the long-term running of the Centre has very little relevance to the planning process. The documented Plan has almost no reference to the problem since it is irrelevant to anyone reviewing the plans of the School.

The Centre had identified several problems that could affect the outcome of the target. Each was considered separately. It was felt that possible problems that could occur if the Centre exceeded its plans were a low risk in the environment at the time of writing the Plan. As such, the document did not waste time exploring the effects of this outcome.However, the opposite could not also be said to be true. If turnover were to drop, the Centre would have to take action to compensate. The Centre was sufficiently strong that the actions that would need to be taken could be restricted to cutting out the higher-risk areas of its proposed development. However, all possibilities were considered. In the event of turnover being less than targeted, the Centre considered how it would react and put in place contingency plans. These were not explained in detail in the Plan since they detract from the longer-term goals of the document. The main goals were to establish a clear focus of the proposed direction of the Centre for management and staff, and to provide objective benchmarks against which to test whether the principles in the Plan were working.

There were a number of detailed problems which the management had identified as needing to be dealt with. These included increasing the benefit derived from costs of renting rooms, reducing costs of catering at courses, and how to exploit the geographical position of the Centre in the Barbican. Several alternatives were thrashed out and conclusions reached. These could have been added to the document of the Plan, but the points were too routine. It was felt that their inclusion would not add to the reader's understanding in any material way, but this level of detail could guide the reader into an excessively detailed review of the business. The blend of detailed and general problems could have been substantially changed, depending on who was intended to read the document.

The Plan was aimed primarily at formally summarizing the proposals of the management. The Plan will be shown to all key personnel to ensure they are explicitly aware of the overall objectives. Secondly, it was aimed at the University. The purpose was to ensure they were aware of the plans: if the Centre failed to achieve its turnover, it wanted to ensure it was judged by reference to the longer-term objectives. It was hoped this would ease short-term profit pressures in favour of the longer-term expansion objectives. Without this expansion, the Centre's profits could not be enhanced to the extent required by the University.

Du Boulay Construction Limited

Du Boulay is involved in construction. Its activities are set out succinctly in the Business Plan document. The Plan was written for the construction industry at the start of a recession of almost, for the construction industry, unparalleled degree. The company was extremely ambitious. It had some very good contacts and very loyal customers. This was one of the benefits of having provided a high-quality service in the past. Customers could ill afford, in the recession, to have building works completed late or to anything less than an excellent standard. Du Boulay's work, after all, provided the finishing touches to the appearance of the building and was the first thing seen by the customer's customer.

Many of the Du Boulay's previous customers were facing severe financial problems and had been cutting back on development work. Despite all this, Du Boulay's turnover in the four months to April 1991 were the best on record. But forward orders were not as strong.

In the substantial growth phase of the last eighteenth months, Du Boulay had geared up for increased demand. Now, the reducing demand threatened to plunge the company into a loss position, since the overheads were running at a fixed level.

The pre-document stage of the Plan was interesting – and heated. The directors wanted to continue to expand and had initially targeted growth of 30% over the previous year. This was at a time when many of Du Boulay's competitors were suffering a 50% reduction in the level of business. The Plan was bold. But the contingency planning showed the company going bankrupt if turnover fell by, say, 20% at a time when they were gearing up for a turnover increase of 30%. Their main problem was they had used up all their personal assets to fund recent growth and a catastrophic bad debt two years previously. They had no further funds to fall back on if they lost money. This caused them to curtail some of the growth plan. None of this was mentioned in the document, because it would have been irrelevant.

In the final event, the company chose to take a more prudent route. It looked at cutting costs to provide for a reduced turnover, more in line with forward orders at the time. It looked at all areas of its activities and came up with many creative cost-cutting methods. It then planned to grow. But the Directors were aware of the risk and intended to monitor subsequent performances closely against the Plan, to alert themselves as early as possible to potential problems. It was resolved that they would adopt the contingency plan sooner rather than later if the growth became uncertain.

In view of the significance of the alternatives, the Plan could not omit a reasonably detailed discussion about the contingency. However, little was mentioned about the alternative proposals that could be actioned, once the contingency Plan had been chosen. There would be nothing to stop some of the alternatives being followed if they proved better than the chosen contingency Plan, and inclusion in the report would prove to be unnecessary.

Du Boulay's marketplace is very well established. It is a mature market with extensive competition. The market is so large that Du Boulay are an insignificant part of it. If the market contracted, that would not necessarily cause Du Boulay to contract, as proved by recent trading. Similarly, if the market grew, Du Boulay could not be guaranteed a part of the growth. Therefore, the Market and Competition sections in the Business Plan are very restricted. They are intended to show the reader merely what Du Boulay think will affect them as a company. They do not give much additional information about whether Du Boulay's plans are realistic or not. A detailed market analysis is, therefore, not important.

Du Boulay has another, rather touching, difference from the 'typical' model for the Business Plan. Almost all of the key staff had joined the company straight from the school or higher education. This meant they had little experience to show off in a personnel section. So the section has been adapted. Instead of showing the companies that each of the individuals has worked for, their strengths and specializations were summarized. This resolved the problem of a reader needing to understand how the personnel within the organization are qualified to do the job, with no prior experience to fall back on.

The Plan mentions the precariousness of Du Boulay, given the downturn in the economy and in a market where those competitors that are still in existence are tendering for contracts at below cost to keep them going until the next upturn. The purpose of planning in this case is to see the effect this has on Du Boulay. This helps the company establish a pricing policy and to determine in which direction it should proceed.

The Business Plan does not go beyond six months into the budgeted financial year as it was difficult to assess the turnover as contracts have been sought under intense competition. It was, therefore, essential in these circumstances to ensure that costs were well forecast so that it is possible to know exactly what turnover has to be achieved to at least break even or to take other early management decisions.

20 City University Business School: Management Development Centre Plan

CONTENTS

APPENDICES

1. Organization Details

Trading Address	Frobisher Crescent Barbican Centre London EC2Y 8HB
Business School Council	Sir Peter Graham OBE C R P Brook Mrs Ann Burdus J G W Davies OBE Sir Graham Day C Brandon Gough The Rt Hon The Lord Howie of Troon Sir Peter Miller Christopher Reeves D J Trevelyan CB
Bankers	National Westminster Bank PLC 15 Bishopsgate London EC2P 2AP
Solicitors	Crossman Block Aldwych House Aldwych London WC2B 4HN
Auditors	BDO Binder Hamlyn 20 Old Bailey EC4M 7BH

2. Summary of Plan

The Management Development Centre is a training organization. It is a centre within the City University Business School. Our objectives are becoming increasingly profit-motivated. The Centre aims to expand its activities over the next few years by following the strategy set out below. The Centre's trading activities are set out in Section 3.

The Centre has been reasonably profitable. Its profits for the year ended 30 September 1990 were £80,000, from turnover of £1.3 million. The Centre expects to make a small loss during the year ending 30 September 1991. The trading history is described in more detail in Section 4.

The Centre operates in a reasonably fragmented market, which has grown considerably over the past few years. The market is described in Section 5.

We believe the market will expand over the next four years for reasons set out in Section 8. We plan to expand out own activities by growing on the back of an expanded market. We are also adopting a number of activities which should allow a modest increase in our market share. Section 9 sets out these plans.

The financial consequences of the growth plan over the next two years are detailed in Section 10. Our forecasts indicate this growth will provide increased profitability. We expect to continue to have a positive cash flow throughout this growth. This reflects the industry's standard policy of invoicing in advance of providing lectures.

3. Activities

The Centre provides business education and training. The school is part of the City University and was set up to specialize in Business courses. The Management Development Centre's reporting requirements are becoming increasingly autonomous. There are increasing pressures on profitability performance. This document sets out the Centre's plans to improve its profitability.

Courses cover two main areas. These are Professional qualifications and Management skills.

a) Professional qualifications

The main qualifications currently taught are:

General Securities Representatives, Securities Industry Diploma Society of Investment Analysts

These courses are all run in the evenings, and have larger than average class sizes. They have direct competition which constrains the fee level.

b) Business skills

The courses cover amongst other things:

Management skills (e.g. Effective Presenting)
Technical Education/Update (e.g. Fund management techniques)
Finance/Accounting (e.g. Using Company Accounts)
Law (e.g. The Essentials of Company Law)
Economics (e.g. Economics for Dealers)
Personal Skills (e.g. The Well-Organized Manager)
Background understanding (e.g. Understanding the City)

The courses fall into two main categories:

i. Public course training

These cover a wide range of business topics. They cover law, internal audit, management skills, finance and accounting and others. They are advertised by direct mail. The number of delegates on a course can range from 5 to 200. We specialize in courses of restricted size to allow participation.

Prices are dependent on competition, but less so than the Qualification courses.

Public courses represent about two-thirds of the Centre's activities.

ii   *Tailor-made courses (called In House training)*

These are designed to meet the requirements of an individual company. The number of delegates varies from 10 to 300. The courses are marketed by direct contact with prospective clients.

The prices are less responsive to competitive pressures and tend to result in regular business each year. This is because they require more specialized skill to design the most effective content and to select the most appropriate lecturers to suit the requirements of the individual client.

We have been successful at graduate training level (Morgan Grenfell, Bank of England, Japanese Bank Consortium for example) and in the field of management. We are very pleased that we have recently won a contract for a high-level management development programme for a major construction company. The value of this contract is expected to realize in excess of £100,000.

c)   *Geographical area of operation*

The Centre operates mainly from the Barbican in the City of London. We use the Trade Centre and offices of Ernst and Young in Dubai to offer public programmes in the Gulf. Before the Gulf War, it made reasonable contributions to the activities of the Centre. During the current year, this business has substantially curtailed. There has been a recent pick-up which has partially recovered the position this year.

The vast majority of participants on courses run in the City come from the UK. The majority of those come from City institutions. A small number of participants come from outside the UK. During the current year, the number of overseas participants has also decreased from previous years.

d)   *Clientele*

The Centre has a good spread of clients. No one client accounts for more than 5% of total turnover.

The Centre has a prestigious client list. Clients include the Bank of England, Midland Bank, Jones Lang Wooton, Nikko Securities, James Capel, Extel, British Telecom, Routledge, Sainsbury's and many other household names.

4. History

a) Background

The Centre was set up around 15 years ago as a specialized unit within the City University Business School. Commercial pressures were placed on the Centre increasingly. In 1985, Phillippa Bourne, a commercial manager, was recruited to develop a semi-independent profit centre of the University.

During the last six years, marketing and accounting systems have been introduced on an increasingly commercial basis.

b) Past results

Accounting for the Centre's activities was historically the responsibility of the University. All payments are made by the University and income is remitted immediately on receipt. Certain costs are incurred by the University. These are increasingly being charged to the Centre. Because the basis of recharge has been inconsistent, comparison of previous year's performance is difficult. The summary of results over the last five years is set out in Appendix I. An attempt has been made to adjust the results to achieve consistency, but care must be taken in interpreting the trends.

The key trends are (£'000):

Year ended 30 September:

	1987	1988	1989	1990	1991 (projected)
Sales	767	905	1,047	1,316	1,322
Gross profit	334	427	455	530	553
Surplus	19	61	71	80	(34)

c) Analysis of trends

The 1991 and 1992 years are expected to show a slowdown reflecting the recession. But the long-term trends are expected to improve for reasons set out in Section 6. The Gulf War caused an identified loss of business in the year ended 30 September 1991 which is not expected to be repeated in future years.

d) Other points

Because the Centre is part of the City University, we are unable to recover VAT paid. The estimated cost to the Centre is £100,000 in the year ending 30 September 1991.

We are investigating whether the Centre can be restructured to enable VAT to be recovered. The benefit of this recovery has not been reflected in this Plan.

Financial pressures on all Universities have been increasing over the last few years. No reflection has been made in the Plan to reflect any changes in accounting or cost allocation the University may require from the Centre.

During the current year, we have lost the IBM In House courses due to the recession.

A number of new In House clients have been added to our list. These include Routledge, Richard Ellis, DKB, Extel, Citicorp, Withers Solicitors and Korean National Bank. Some public courses have been introduced. 'Essentials of Corporate Finance' and 'Essentials of Financial Markets' were particularly successful. In addition, we have had two successful collaborative ventures, one with the National Health Service which attracted over 200 delegates and a two-day high-level course run in conjunction with Bain Management Consultants.

We further ran a successful two-day conference in conjunction with Hoskyns. The conference was presented by top-level speakers, including Sir Colin Marshall and Edward de Bono.

Numbers attending the Securities and Industry Programme in Autumn were very low but picked up during the year. The programme should show an increased surplus. The number of Home Study Packs (participants studying courses remotely from their own home) has grown to bring an increase of over £20,000 this year.

5 Marketplace and Marketing

5.1 The Market

The market is supplied by four types of organizations. These are:

Academic organizations, such as Universities

Younger, growing private institutions

Many small organizations, not much more than individuals

Internal training

The market is well fragmented. No single training organization dominates the market. We estimate that the top ten organizations account for no more than 50% of the overall training market.

Similarly, no single customer has a significant share of demand. The pattern and nature of demand is changing. But we believe the demand is spread among companies in relation to the number of their employees.

The market demand comes from:

Individuals taking personal qualifications

Large corporations sending personnel on improvement courses

Large corporations using outside training centres to improve and supplement their internal training facilities

Small and medium-sized corporations who want to train their staff. Typically, they do not have the resources to set up their own training departments but require the facility.

5.2 Market position

The Centre has positioned itself at the high-quality end of the market. In particular, some of our distinguishing features are:

a) Use of high-quality teachers. We tend to pay a little above the market norm for trainers, which helps attract the better trainers.

b) The courses are designed with a high-quality content. Care and time is taken designing courses over and above the average, to ensure all practical aspects of a particular subject are covered.

c) The class sizes are intentionally small. This allows personal involvement. We believe this makes the courses more effective and more enjoyable.

d) We are perceived by the market to be strong in practical development but weak in technical skills. The perception is wrong. The Centre's academic background ensures we are strong technically. This misconception may provide us with future opportunities.

e) There is one area of courses in which we are weak. Various larger corporations have a two- to four-week residential course to improve management capability, at a particular stage of development of potential managers. Some of these corporations contract out the courses. They are developed over a number of years and are specific to that company. The courses are developed with a very high amount of input by the client company.

This is a very profitable market. But it is one in which we have had no real involvement in the past. We believe it would be expensive to try to break into these markets in the short run. We plan to increase general market awareness of the Centre. When this is achieved, it is expected we will begin to take some of this market when people who have attended our courses ask us to do increasingly specialized In House training. As this side of the business develops, we will be increasingly able to provide a specific structured series of training at this level of management.

5.3 Marketing strategy

Courses are publicized almost exclusively by direct mail. It is the experience of course providers that this is the most cost effective way. The major exception is promotion of evening qualification courses where advertising in National and London papers has been effective, especially in conjunction with a direct mail campaign.

The operation at present involves production of an annual brochure of public courses sent to about 15,000 people listed on the Centre's own database. This is supplemented by leaflets for each course sent to a specific target audience. The leaflets are relatively inexpensive. They are sent out in batches of 5 to 7 per envelope to interested groups. The response rate per course is about 0.3%. The average marketing cost per delegate varies enormously according to the course, but the average marketing cost per course is £1,100 – about one-third of the total cost of the course. The percentage of total cost per course spent on marketing is, therefore, much higher for a one-day course than for a longer course.

The Centre's mailing list database has been considerably improved. It now has close to 15,000 names and addresses. Each is coded by job title and organization. Our own lists are supplemented by lists bought from commercial list brokers. Analysis is constantly being carried out to find the most responsive lists.

The timing of course publicity is critical to its success. If the mailing is too early or late, it has a clearly adverse effect on the number of bookings. We have tight schedules worked out with our printers and mailers. The system at present seems to be working well.

Marketing of tailor-made programmes has tended to be more passive in the past. We have relied on organizations approaching us to discuss their training requirements. We now plan to be more active in the future to stimulate new business. This is described in more detail in Section 9.

5.4 Market function

The main function within the market is training.

The benefit of using the Management Development Centre over self-training or competitors depends on the type of training requirements of the client organization.

a) *Public courses*

The Centre is able to promote specific and specialized courses. By having a good awareness of developments within both the general economy and specific industries, the Centre is able to research subjects and spread the cost over several participants.

Because of the number of courses given, the Centre is able to allocate several courses to presenters or lecturers. This helps attract the best people and commands a degree of loyalty. By using the lecturers on many occasions, the Centre is able to identify the strengths and weaknesses of each lecturer. We can ensure that the best lecturer is used for each course. This exploits their strengths and ensures they are not used to give courses where their weaknesses would be exposed.

The administrative effort of arranging a course is considerable. The Centre has developed very efficient systems which reduce the cost to a minimum. If organizations implement their own training schemes, these administrative costs are incurred and may be more costly than those incurred by the Centre.

b) *In House training*

The Centre's breadth of expertise ensures that it is aware of all current developments within an Industry. When an organization is presenting an In House course, the Centre is able to ensure all the relevant current developments are covered and that the most appropriate lecturer is available. The

Centre's expertise with lecturers almost guarantees that In House courses are improved if the Centre is involved.

c) *Professional qualification courses*

The Centre provides training to a nationally approved standard. The size and organization allows us to provide facilities for qualification courses which allow individuals to obtain professional qualifications.

d) *Prestige*

The Centre has a certain degree of prestige which internal and small organizations lack. This is useful to companies as a recruitment incentive for potential employees. Therefore, the attraction of using the City University Business Centre is greater than using many competitors.

e) *Geographic location*

The Centre is situated in the Barbican, in the heart of the City of London. Therefore, the Centre has an advantage over its competitors in that City organizations can release staff for courses which are within easy reach of their office. The costs of travel are eliminated and the familiarity of surroundings is often seen as a psychological advantage in choosing a course.

6 Competition

As explained in Section 5, the market is divided into four categories of suppliers. We believe competition from the small organizations is not relevant to the Centre. The areas in which clients have to choose between a larger and smaller organization have a short-term effect only. Therefore, the review of competition is restricted to competitors of comparable size and status.

a) London Business School

Three-day and longer programmes. High quality and towards the higher end of the price range. Competition on City/Finance courses e.g. Corporate Finance. Have residential facilities.

Their 1989–90 turnover from Business subjects was £3.2m. for Executive Programme fees and £1.4m for In House training.

b) Ashridge

Three-day and longer programmes; high quality and expensive. Less competitive on Finance/City courses but more on Management development and Marketing. Excellent residential facilities. Supplement own faculty with visiting staff.

c) Henley Management College

Provide distance learning packs trading as BTN Henley, for Securities Industry courses as well as some longer Management development programmes. Excellent residential facilities.

d) Manchester Business School

Direct competitors on In House banking courses – in spite of their location. Also offering Public courses.

e) Hawkesmere/Euromoney/Economist/FT

Mainly perceived as conference organizers for large groups. Their pricing is towards the higher end of the market. Direct competition on City and Finance courses in terms of subjects. We understand they use almost exclusively visiting speakers and practitioners.

f) Financial Training

Direct competitors in Securities Industry and Society of Investment Analysts course. Also run In House finance courses and, recently, a small number of Public courses. They have a good reputation as 'crammers' and have a good pass rate.

Owned by Wolters Kluwer. The group has worldwide training income of £60m. The UK activities represent about 12% of the worldwide training and non-training activities.

g) Mobile Training

Aiming at the lower end of the market, they are less expensive than most. Undertake some In House training for some of our clients.

h) D C Gardner

Direct competitors on both public and In House City and Finance training. Good reputation. They have recently developed their own residential facilities.

Their training and publishing section had joint turnover of £17m. for the year ended 31 December 1990, of which £1.7m. related to residential training centres.

i) Cranfield School of Management

The School's core activities are the provision of MBA degrees. Their Business School aims at similar markets as we do. They claim to be presenting 300 courses per annum at which they have 4,500 participants.

j) Professional Institutes (e.g. CIMA, ICAEW, IIA, BIM)

Direct competition of short Public courses. Slightly less expensive than us.

CIMA's 1990 turnover was £885,000 from management courses.

k) Individuals

Competition for In House courses. With few overheads, they are much less expensive than the larger organizations. Any one trainer tends to have specialist and restricted expertise.

7. Personnel

The key personnel are:

a) Phillippa Bourne BA MBA MCIM MBIM (Managing Director)

Responsible for the overall direction of the Centre. Includes responsibility for expanding the activities and profitability of the Centre and for enhancing its reputation. She has been working at the Management Development Centre for six years, initially as General Manager, then as Director.

Before this, she worked as Technical Director for Management Education with the Chartered Institute of Management Accountants with responsibility for developing and running their short course programme. Previous experience has been in marketing. This included analysis with Serck Baker, specialists in water treatment equipment for the oil industry. Also worked for Telehoist Limited, manufacturers of tipping gear for commercial vehicles and Killick Martin Limited, shipbrokers.

Phillippa Bourne has an MBA with a marketing speciality.

b) Dr Alan Webber BA

Alan is a Financial Markets Courses Director in the Centre.

His responsibilities include planning and implementing programmes of new and existing financial markets courses, devising new courses and finding lecturers.

He has an academic background in relation to banking and finance, monetary and economic history. He is the author of a major book and writes articles and discussion papers. He earned a BA in History in 1976, and a PhD in Economic and Social Science in 1982. He currently teaches the third-year undergraduates' course Financial Markets, and Stock Exchange Examination courses. He has taught Introduction to Money, Banking and International Finance and Monetary History classes. He also teaches on all types of the Management Development Centre finance courses.

c) Sarah Karslake

Sarah's function is to manage the running of the Centre's courses, to develop new courses and to contribute towards the general management and business development of the Centre.

She has a degree is Business Studies. She joined the Centre in 1985 as Course Organizer with responsibility for administration and co-ordination of a number of designated courses. In 1988, she became Courses Manager, with responsibility for all administrative matters of all events run by the Centre. Functions include staff recruitment and management, dealing with course evaluations and liaison with lecturers following feedback, meeting new clients and controlling movement and use of equipment.

d) Javed Ishaq

Javed is responsible for the Financial accounting of the Centre. He has been responsible for implementing all the financial systems that are currently in place.

He joined the school two years ago, coming from Coverfield Limited, an insurance company, where he was responsible for production of management and statutory accounts.

e) Ash Kotecha BSc MBA

Ash is the newest member of the management team, joining in November 1990. He was recruited as the Marketing Manager. He has an MBA with a specialism in Marketing.

After graduation in 1986, he took up a post of marketing co-ordinator with a jeans manufacturer based in the Midlands. He was responsible for the introduction of a new brand of adults and children's jeans and accessories. His duties included all aspects of supervision of the project from the design conception to production and distribution.

8. Direction of market

The market is in the process of fundamental change. The changes are blurred by the current recession.

8.1 General trend

We believe the overall trend in training is an increase in the markets. The key development seems to be the increased awareness of training as a practical method of improving the skill and performance of staff within an organization. Going hand in hand with this awareness is an increased requirement for 'value for money' training. Client companies and participants increasingly demand to leave a course feeling they have learnt something of practical value.

The trend, therefore, is an increase in the amount of training required. Larger organizations are increasing the training of staff and are increasingly performing the training themselves. The downside risk is that they will send their staff away for courses less than in the past. The upside risk is that they will require increasingly expert external assistance to ensure the quality of their own training is increasingly effective. Whereas there is the scope to use individuals for such training, we believe that the organizations will quickly see a drop in the quality and breadth of courses given internally as the limitations of the individual takes its toll on the course content. We believe that the extra cost per delegate of using larger organizations to enhance the quality of internal courses will be insignificant compared to the extra value, in the long run.

As personnel in the larger organizations become more trained, they will expect and demand more specialist training which will not be cost effective for the organization to run. We believe that specialist courses will have an increasingly important role within the Centre over the next few years.

The same pressures will have a more direct impact on smaller to medium-sized organizations. They want their staff to be trained, but they lack the resources to train them internally. Therefore, we believe that any business lost from larger organizations will be more than made up from increased attendance by smaller and medium-sized organizations.

8.2 Value for money

The 'value for money' approach has caused a trend away from the 'glossy' courses where there are several speakers over a two- to three-day period. The cost will be perceived to be better spent on more tailored and practical training. The 'glossy' courses will not die out, but they will decrease in significance within the market as a whole.

8.3 Distance learning

There is a change to 'distance' learning. This is where courses are presented remotely by correspondence and video. Papers are marked without the lecturer ever meeting the participant. The trend has been slow over recent years, but we believe it may be picking up pace. If this trend continues, it will reduce profitability in the short run, until resources are spread more efficiently to meet the demand. If run efficiently, the 'distance' courses can be far more profitable since facilities are not needed to give the course, and the timing of the training is far more flexible to respond to the specific needs of the individual.

8.4 Smaller training organizations

There is a substantial increase in the number of individuals and small organizations providing training. We believe this trend will continue in view of the low entry cost to the market of providing such services. However, smaller training organizations will find it very difficult to keep up to date with developments in the relative industry. They will have more success in the Personal Skills courses, such as Negotiation Skills and Effective Presentational Skills, than in Industry Related Skills, such as Securities and Investment Board and Understanding Company Accounts. However, the cost of marketing is so high, it is unlikely that many of the smaller organizations will be able to develop profitably outside their restricted field of expertise. Since so much of the attraction of a particular course is based on past experience of the participant with the Centre, the larger organizations will continue to outperform the smaller ones in attracting participants.

8.5 Marketing methods

The final trend which we believe to be the key is the reduced success of direct mailing. It is possible that the trend is caused by the recession. But improved marketing and computer skills of most organizations increase the amount of direct mail. As the level of direct mail increases, so its effectiveness reduces. Alternate methods of direct marketing will become more important in the future. We believe this will improve the performance of the Centre relative to most organizations since we are well placed to carry out alternate direct marketing activities.

9. Strategy and Plans

The key objective of the Centre is to run a profitable organization which provides funds for the University. This will be done by providing courses which are required by the market. This will be achieved by continuing to provide high-quality courses and to enhance the reputation, image and awareness that organizations have of the Centre.

We believe the markets are due to increase over the next few years. Organizations will demand higher-quality courses and will look for enhanced 'value for money' training. More expensive courses will succeed better than cheaper courses if the value for the cost is greater. Therefore, we intend to continue to concentrate on providing high-quality courses and to establish a reputation for quality and practicality. Participants should leave our courses feeling that they have learnt something and that it will be of direct practical value to them. Companies sending staff should see improved performance of staff they send on our courses.

a) Cutting costs

Direct costs cannot be cut without a reduction in the calibre of staff. Marketing costs cannot be cut in real terms without a reduction in bookings. But the longer courses have a lower marketing cost compared with the fee income. Therefore, we intend to increase the emphasis of courses towards longer courses.

Similarly, as the number of delegates per course increases, the fixed cost per delegate decreases. Whereas the Centre will continue to provide the high-quality services for small numbers of private participants, it is intended that the number of participants at Public courses will increase.

Room hire is relatively expensive. However, the cost to the Centre is income to the University. It is proposed to highlight the excess cost to the Centre to ensure the benefit to the University matches the savings that could be achieved if the Centre ran courses in different locations.

b) Marketing

The general aim is to improve the response rate to marketing. We are constantly improving the quality of the database. Analysis is constantly improving our understanding of which are the most responsive mailing lists.

We have collected more information about existing Public course companies. This will enable us to make more effective contact with them, by providing them with better and more direct information about our services which they may benefit from. We are increasing the number of direct visits to existing customers, to develop a closer relationship with them. We expect a number of In House courses to result from these visits.

We have recently introduced the concept of season tickets. This involves organizations being able to buy a block of training. The main benefit is the strengthening of links with customers and the increased number of bookings from each firm.

The brochures are being redesigned to highlight the key points of interest of each course – and to make the reader aware of some of the excellent feedback we have been getting from courses recently.

New courses are being developed which directly follow on from existing courses. This should enable us to market new courses at courses being given – marketing costs of these courses would be reduced.

We will run large 'conference' type events in conjunction with other organizations. This should allow us to tap into their database which are likely to be more targeted and accurate. We should also be able to achieve a degree of marketing at no extra cost by utilizing the existing communication facilities of the organization.

c) Scope of courses

We will aim to provide more In House courses. This can be achieved by more targeted marketing. We will be contacting customers directly to find out about their requirements. This will ensure courses are constantly updated to include those subjects, and it will provide a logical development into In House training if the customer has that need.

We are looking into developing Insurance courses. These would fit in well with our City courses, both from the perspective of experience and contacts.

d) Pricing

Our prices are higher than several of our competitors, although there is a significant number of Business Schools that are more expensive than we are. We believe the value we give, however, is correspondingly higher. By continually improving the quality and content of courses, we should be able to charge higher prices. This can be achieved by moving into more specialized In House markets.

e) Technical ability

The Centre is incorrectly perceived as being weak on technical subjects. Marketing will concentrate on rectifying this misconception. This should increase the number of people attending some of the courses provided by the Centre.

f) VAT

Under the present legal system, the Centre is unable to recover the VAT it spends. It is estimated that this costs the school in the region of £100,000 per annum. The Centre will explore with the University ways in which the problem could be remedied. This would have an immediate and direct impact on profits.

10   Financial Forecasts

The detailed profit and loss and cash flow forecasts are set out in the appendices.

In view of the recession, the forecasts were carried out on three bases. One sets out the Plan. One assumes that turnover is 10% lower than planned. The final forecast assumes turnover will drop by 25% from forecast. Since the Centre has a positive working capital flow, it was considered unnecessary to look at the possibility of turnover increasing beyond the Plan.

a) Profitability

	Plan	Plan less 10%	Plan less 25%
	£'000	£'000	£'000
Year ending 30 September 1992			
Turnover	1,513	1,361	1,134
Gross profits	643	579	482
Overheads	627	580	532
Net profits	16	(1)	(50)
Year ending 30 September 1993			
Turnover	1,780	1,600	1,335
Gross profits	765	688	590
Overheads	659	605	570
Net profits	106	83	20

b) Cash flow funding

A series of cash flow forecasts were prepared on different assumptions. The table below summarizes three financial consequences of different scenarios. The scenarios are achieving target, falling 10% below target and falling 25% below target. We believe the risk of falling more than 25% below target to be very remote.

The key consequences summarized below are:

i   Fixed assets. It is assumed they will not change, independent of achievement.

ii The working capital surplus during the period. This represents money received in advance from courses less the amount due to consultants, lecturers and in payment of overheads. Because of the industry's pricing policy, the working capital produces a positive cash inflow to the business. The figure set out in the table below is the minimum cash inflow at any time during the year forecast.

iii The net funding flow is the net bank overdraft plus borrowings plus balance due to the Business School. The figure set out in the table below is the maximum funding requirement at any time during the year forecast.

	Plan	Plan less 10%	Plan less 25%
	£'000	£'000	£'000
Fixed assets required	50	50	50
Working capital surplus (minimum)	47	26	13
Net funding flow (maximum)	70	97	122

Note – It is assumed that the Centre will cut some of its development plans if turnover falls below the Plan. In this way, the longer-term development of the Centre will be slowed, but funds will be released to compensate for lost turnover.

The Centre has arranged facilities of £122,000 to cover the maximum funding flow, if it is required.

CITY UNIVERSITY BUSINESS SCHOOL PLAN
DETAILED PROJECTED PROFIT & LOSS ACCOUNT
FOR THE YEAR ENDED
31 September 1991

Appendix I

£'000	Forecast Year to 31/9/91	Projected Year to 31/9/91	Forecast Year to 31/9/92
SALES	1,332	1,322	1,513
COST OF SALES			
Purchases	772	769	870
GROSS PROFIT	560	553	643
GROSS PROFIT PER CENT	42.0%	41.8%	42.5%
OVERHEADS			
Admin/Accounts staff	286	333	340
Publicity	75	70	75
Equipment	12	12	13
Photocopying	20	20	21
Printing/Stationery	33	25	35
Conference/Travel	1	1	1
Hospitality	2	2	2
Set up costs: New courses	5	5	5
Postage/Telephone	13	11	14
Miscellaneous	8	6	8
Accounting fees	17	17	24
Other overheads	4	4	8
Contrib. to Level 11	21	21	21
Contrib. to Level 12	60	60	60
	557	587	627
OPERATING PROFIT	3	−34	16

CITY UNIVERSITY BUSINESS SCHOOL PLAN   Appendix II
HISTORIC PROFIT & LOSS ACCOUNT
FOR THE FIVE YEARS ENDED
31 September 1990

£'000	Year to 31/9/86	Year to 31/9/87	Year to 31/9/88	Year to 31/9/89	Year to 31/9/90
SALES	564	767	905	1,047	1,316
COST OF SALES					
Purchases	275	433	478	592	786
GROSS PROFIT	289	334	427	455	530
GROSS PROFIT PER CENT	51.2%	43.5%	47.2%	43.5%	40.3%
OVERHEADS					
Admin and central costs		254	305	323	373
Accommodation costs		61	61	61	77
		315	366	384	450
OPERATING PROFIT		19	61	71	80

CITY UNIVERSITY BUSINESS SCHOOL PLAN   Appendix III
PROJECTED PROFIT & LOSS ACCOUNT
FOR THE FIVE YEARS ENDED
31 September 1995

£'000	Year to 31/9/91	Year to 31/9/92	Year to 31/9/93	Year to 31/9/94	Year to 31/9/95
SALES	1,332	1,513	1,780	2,022	2,246
COST OF SALES					
Purchases	779	870	1,015	1,142	1,303
GROSS PROFIT	553	643	765	880	943
GROSS PROFIT PER CENT	41.5%	42.5%	43.0%	43.5%	42.0%
OVERHEADS					
Admin/Accounts staff	338	350	370	400	430
Marketing	70	75	79	79	83
Other costs	77	100	108	116	121
TUC overheads	21	21	21	21	21
Accommodation costs	81	81	81	81	81
	587	627	659	697	736
OPERATING PROFIT	−34	16	106	183	207

CITY UNIVERSITY BUSINESS SCHOOL PLAN

PROJECTED PROFIT & LOSS ACCOUNT
FOR THE YEAR ENDED
31 September 1991

£'000	Oct. 1990	Nov.	Dec.	Jan. 1991	Feb.	March	April	May	June	July	August	Sept.	Total
SALES	118	134	89	104	105	117	123	107	105	110	90	120	1,322
COST OF SALES													
Purchases	67	76	55	64	61	67	70	61	62	63	54	69	769
GROSS PROFIT	51	58	34	40	44	50	53	46	43	47	36	51	553
GROSS PROFIT PER CENT	43%	43%	38%	38%	42%	43%	43%	43%	41%	43%	40%	43%	42%
OVERHEADS													
Cash payments	51	39	39	43	46	40	46	45	41	42	42	42	516
Depreciation	5	6	6	6	6	6	6	6	6	6	6	6	71
	56	45	45	49	52	46	52	51	47	48	48	48	587
OPERATING PROFIT	−5	13	−11	−9	−8	4	1	−5	−4	−1	−12	3	−34
TAXATION													0
NET PROFIT	−5	13	−11	−9	−8	4	1	−5	−4	−1	−12	3	−34

CITY UNIVERSITY BUSINESS SCHOOL PLAN

OVERHEADS
FOR THE YEAR ENDED
31 September 1991

£'000	Oct. 1990	Nov.	Dec.	Jan. 1991	Feb.	March	April	May	June	July	August	Sept.	Total
ADMINISTRATION													
Rent	6.8	6.8	6.8	6.8	6.8	6.8	6.8	6.7	6.6	6.7	6.7	6.7	81.0
Wages & salaries	19.7	19.7	19.7	19.7	19.7	19.7	19.7	19.7	19.7	19.7	19.7	19.7	236.4
National insurance	2.0	2.0	2.0	2.0	2.1	2.0	2.1	2.1	2.1	2.1	2.1	2.1	24.7
Audit & accountancy	1.4	1.4	1.4	1.4	1.4	1.4	1.4	1.4	1.4	1.4	1.5	1.5	17.0
Telephone & Postage	1.1	1.1	1.1	0.9	0.9	0.9	1.4	1.4	1.4	1.1	1.0	1.1	13.4
Printing & Stationery	2.3	2.4	1.7	1.8	2.9	2.1	2.4	2.0	1.7	2.0	2.0	2.0	25.3
Photocopying	1.8	1.9	1.4	1.6	1.9	1.9	1.7	1.6	1.4	1.7	1.7	1.6	20.2
Equipment	0.0	0.0	2.3	1.1	0.2	0.4	2.1	1.6	1.0	1.0	1.0	1.0	11.7
Other expenses	0.7	1.1	1.3	0.9	0.5	0.8	0.6	1.3	0.8	0.9	0.9	1.0	10.8
	35.8	36.4	37.7	36.2	36.4	36.0	38.2	37.8	36.1	36.6	36.6	36.7	440.5
SELLING & DISTRIBUTION													
Marketing	14.7	2.1	1.3	5.8	9.3	3.6	7.5	6.5	4.0	5.0	5.0	5.0	69.8
	14.7	2.1	1.3	5.8	9.3	3.6	7.5	6.5	4.0	5.0	5.0	5.0	69.8
FINANCIAL													
Bank charges													0.0
Bank interest 13%	0.2	0.1	0.0	0.8	0.5	0.5	0.6	0.4	0.3	0.7	0.6	0.5	5.2
	0.2	0.1	0.0	0.8	0.5	0.5	0.6	0.4	0.3	0.7	0.6	0.5	5.2
TOTAL	50.7	38.6	39.0	42.8	46.2	40.1	46.3	44.7	40.4	42.3	42.2	42.2	515.5

CITY UNIVERSITY BUSINESS SCHOOL PLAN

PROJECTED CASH FLOW
FOR THE YEAR ENDED
31 September 1991

£'000	Oct. 1990	Nov.	Dec.	Jan. 1991	Feb.	March	April	May	June	July	August	Sept.	Total
RECEIPTS													
From debtors	99	125	129	102	100	104	114	121	112	105	109	96	1,316
OTHER													0
	99	125	129	102	100	104	114	121	112	105	109	96	1,316
PAYMENTS													
To creditors	73	75	58	63	62	65	70	62	62	63	55	67	775
Overheads	51	39	39	43	46	40	46	45	41	42	42	42	516
Prepayments/(Accruals)	-51	-11	56	-28	-12	3	-18	9	15	-14	12	-20	-59
CAPITAL EXPENDITURE													
Plant and equipment	10	10	5	5									30
Furniture & fittings	3	7											10
Motor vehicles			7										7
Other assets		3											3
DISTRIBUTIONS			30						30				60
	86	123	195	83	96	108	98	116	148	91	109	89	1,342
Net movement	13	2	-66	19	4	-4	16	5	-36	14	0	7	-26
Balance b/f	-19	-6	-4	-70	-51	-47	-51	-35	-30	-66	-52	-52	-19
Balance c/f	-6	-4	-70	-51	-47	-51	-35	-30	-66	-52	-52	-45	-45

147

CITY UNIVERSITY BUSINESS SCHOOL PLAN

PROJECTED BALANCE SHEET
FOR THE YEAR ENDED
31 September 1991

£'000	Opening Balance	Oct. 1990	Nov.	Dec.	Jan. 1991	Feb.	March	April	May	June	July	August	Sept.
FIXED ASSETS													
Cost	240	253	273	285	290	290	290	290	290	290	290	290	290
Depreciation	-57	-62	-68	-74	-80	-86	-92	-98	-104	-110	-116	-122	-122
	183	191	205	211	210	204	198	192	186	180	174	168	168
CURRENT ASSETS													
Debtors	141	160	169	129	131	136	149	158	144	137	142	123	147
Prepayments/(Accruals)	-53	-104	-115	-59	-87	-99	-96	-114	-105	-90	-104	-92	-112
Bank & cash	0	0	0	0	0	0	0	0	0	0	0	0	0
Other	2	2	2	2	2	2	2	2	2	2	2	2	2
	90	58	56	72	46	39	55	46	41	49	40	33	37
CURRENT LIABILITIES													
Overdraft	-19	-6	-4	-70	-51	-47	-51	-35	-30	-66	-52	-52	-45
Trade creditors	-16	-10	-11	-8	-9	-8	-10	-10	-9	-9	-9	-8	-10
Sundry creditors	-3	-3	-3	-3	-3	-3	-3	-3	-3	-3	-3	-3	-9
	-38	-19	-18	-81	-63	-58	-64	-48	-42	-78	-64	-63	-64
NET ASSETS	235	230	243	202	193	185	189	190	185	151	150	138	141
SHARE CAPITAL	0	0	0	0	0	0	0	0	0	0	0	0	0
RETAINED RESERVES													
Opening	235	235	230	243	202	193	185	189	190	185	151	150	138
Profit for month		-5	13	-11	-9	-8	4	1	-5	-4	1	-1	-12	3
less: Distributions		0	0	30	0	0	0	0	0	0	-30	0	0	0
	235	230	243	202	193	190	190	185	151	150	138	141	
	235	230	243	202	193	185	190	190	185	151	150	138	141

NOTES TO THE PROJECTIONS
FOR THE YEAR ENDED
31 September 1991

£'000
1. DEBTORS

	Oct. 1990	Nov.	Dec.	Jan. 1991	Feb.	March	April	May	June	July	August	Sept.	Total
B/f	141	160	169	129	131	136	149	158	144	137	142	123	141
Sales	118	134	89	104	105	117	123	107	105	110	90	120	1,322
VAT	0	0	0	0	0	0	0	0	0	0	0	0	0
Cash received	−99	−125	−129	−102	−100	−104	−114	−121	−112	−105	−109	−96	−1,316
C/f	160	169	129	131	136	149	158	144	137	142	123	147	147

NOTES TO THE PROJECTIONS (Cont.)—
REPAYMENT PROFILE

	Opening Balance	Oct. 1990	Nov.	Dec.	Jan. 1991	Feb.	March	April	May	June	July	August	Sept.
Month 0	70%	0%	0%	0%	0%	0%	0%	0%	0%	0%	0%	0%	0%
Month 1	30%	70%	70%	70%	70%	70%	70%	70%	70%	70%	70%	70%	70%
Month 2	0%	30%	30%	30%	30%	30%	30%	30%	30%	30%	30%	30%	30%
Month 3	0%	0%	0%	0%	0%	0%	0%	0%	0%	0%	0%	0%	0%
Month 4	0%	0%	0%	0%	0%	0%	0%	0%	0%	0%	0%	0%	0%
Total	100%	100%	100%	100%	100%	100%	100%	100%	100%	100%	100%	100%	100%

2. CREDITORS

	Oct. 1990	Nov.	Dec.	Jan. 1991	Feb.	March	April	May	June	July	August	Sept.	Total
B/f	16	10	11	8	9	8	10	10	9	9	9	8	16
Purchases (incl. VAT)	67	76	55	64	61	67	70	61	62	63	54	69	769
VAT	0	0	0	0	0	0	0	0	0	0	0	0	0
Cash paid	−73	−75	−58	−63	−62	−65	−70	−62	−62	−63	−55	−67	−775
C/f	10	11	8	9	8	10	10	9	9	9	8	10	10

NOTES TO THE PROJECTIONS (Cont.)

REPAYMENT PROFILE

	Opening Balance	Oct. 1990	Nov.	Dec.	Jan. 1991	Feb.	March	April	May	June	July	August	Sept.
		Purchases	Purchases	Purchases	Purchases	Purchases	Purchases	Purchases	Purchases	Purchases	Purchases	Purchases	Purchases
Month 0	100%	85%	85%	85%	85%	85%	85%	85%	85%	85%	85%	85%	85%
Month 1	0%	15%	15%	15%	15%	15%	15%	15%	15%	15%	15%	15%	15%
Month 2	0%	0%	0%	0%	0%	0%	0%	0%	0%	0%	0%	0%	0%
Month 3	0%	0%	0%	0%	0%	0%	0%	0%	0%	0%	0%	0%	0%
Month 4	0%	0%	0%	0%	0%	0%	0%	0%	0%	0%	0%	0%	0%
Total	100%	100%	100%	100%	100%	100%	100%	100%	100%	100%	100%	100%	100%

NOTES TO THE PROJECTIONS (Cont.)
SELLING & DISTRIBUTION
Marketing

3. PREPAYMENTS

	Opening Balance	Oct. 1990	Nov.	Dec.	Jan. 1991	Feb.	March	April	May	June	July	August	Sept.
Marketing	25	23	21	19	17	15	13	11	9	7	5	3	1
Rent	12	6	0	12	6	0	12	6	0	12	6	0	12
Other													
Total	37	29	21	31	23	15	25	17	9	19	11	3	13

4. ACCRUALS

	Opening Balance	Oct. 1990	Nov.	Dec.	Jan. 1991	Feb.	March	April	May	June	July	August	Sept.
Marketing	7	15	2	1	6	9	4	8	7	4	5	5	5
Invoicing in advance	83	118	134	89	104	105	117	123	107	105	110	90	120
Other													
	90	133	136	90	110	114	121	131	114	109	115	95	125

Note – It has been assumed that invoicing of customers occurs on average 30 days in advance of the course. Assumptions relating to the payment of invoices is set out in note 1 on debtors

NOTES TO THE PROJECTIONS (Cont.)

RECEIPTS

Other

5. FIXED ASSETS

	Oct. 1990	Nov.	Dec.	Jan. 1991	Feb.	March	April	May	June	July	August	Sept.	Total
PLANT & EQUIPMENT													
Cost:													
B/f	82	92	102	107	112	112	112	112	112	112	112	112	82
Additions	10	10	5	5	0	0	0	0	0	0	0	0	30
Disposals													0
C/f	92	102	107	112	112	112	112	112	112	112	112	112	112
Depreciation:	25%	25%	25%	25%	25%	25%	25%	25%	25%	25%	25%	25%	25%
B/f	14	16	18	20	22	24	26	28	30	33	34	36	14
Charge	2	2	2	2	2	2	2	2	2	2	2	2	24
Disposals													0
C/f	16	18	20	22	24	26	28	30	32	34	36	38	38
Net book value	76	84	87	90	88	86	84	82	80	78	76	74	74
Other													
FURNITURE & FITTINGS													
Cost:													
B/f	113	116	123	123	123	123	123	123	123	123	123	123	113
Additions	3	7	0	0	0	0	0	0	0	0	0	0	10
Disposals													0
C/f	116	123	123	123	123	123	123	123	123	123	123	123	123
Depreciation:	25%	25%	25%	25%	25%	25%	25%	25%	25%	25%	25%	25%	25%
B/f	18	20	23	26	29	32	35	38	41	44	47	50	18
Charge	2	3	3	3	3	3	3	3	3	3	3	3	35
Disposals													0
C/f	20	23	26	29	32	35	38	41	44	47	50	53	53
Net book value	96	100	97	94	91	88	85	82	79	76	73	70	70

NOTES TO THE PROJECTIONS (Cont.)

MOTOR VEHICLES

Cost:													
B/f	35	35	35	42	42	42	42	42	42	42	42	42	35
Additions	0	0	7	0	0	0	0	0	0	0	0	0	7
Disposals													0
C/f	35	35	42	42	42	42	42	42	42	42	42	42	42
Depreciation:	25%	25%	25%	25%	25%	25%	25%	25%	25%	25%	25%	25%	25%
B/f	21	22	23	24	25	26	27	28	29	30	31	32	21
Charge	1	1	1	1	1	1	1	1	1	1	1	1	10
Disposals													0
C/f	22	23	24	25	26	27	28	29	30	31	32	33	33
Net book value	13	12	18	17	16	15	14	13	12	11	10	9	9

OTHER ASSETS

Cost:													
B/f	10	10	13	13	13	13	13	13	13	13	13	13	10
Additions	0	3	0	0	0	0	0	0	0	0	0	0	3
Disposals													0
C/f	10	13	13	13	13	13	13	13	13	13	13	13	13
Depreciation:	25%	25%	25%	25%	25%	25%	25%	25%	25%	25%	25%	25%	25%
B/f	4	4	4	4	4	4	4	4	4	4	4	4	4
Charge	0	0	0	0	0	0	0	0	0	0	0	0	0
Disposals													0
C/f	4	4	4	4	4	4	4	4	4	4	4	4	4
Net book value	6	9	9	9	9	9	9	9	9	9	9	9	9

TOTAL

COST	253	273	285	290	290	290	290	290	290	290	290	290	290
DEPRECIATION	62	68	74	80	86	92	98	104	110	116	122	128	128
NET BOOK VALUE	191	205	211	210	204	198	192	186	180	174	168	162	162

21 Du Boulay Construction Limited Plan

CONTENTS

1 Organization details

2 Summary of Plan

Present position of organization

3 Activities

4 History

5 Marketplace and Marketing

6 Manufacturing

7 Personnel

Future direction and plans of organization

8 Direction of Market

9 Strategy and Plans

APPENDICES [page]

1.   Organization Details

Trading Address   7 Royal Victoria Patriotic Building
                     Fitzhugh Grove
                     London SW18 3SX

Executive Board   D G H du Boulay
                     D C Budd
                     M Reed

Bankers   Barclays Bank PLC
                     Surbiton Business Centre

Solicitors   Compton Carr
                     6 Dyers Buildings
                     Holborn
                     London
                     EC1N 2JT

Auditors   Fairfax & Co
                     Myrtle House
                     Hampton Court
                     Surrey

2. Summary of Plan

Du Boulay Construction Limited was formed in 1976 by the present Financial Director, David Budd and David du Boulay, who himself was experienced in project management, estimating and client liaising for the purposes of commercial property refurbishment.

The Company is looking to ensure that it will continue through the downturn with sufficient working capital and reserves and with a structure such that it will come through the other side with the ability to take on new construction opportunities and move forward with confidence of greater profitability.

3. Activities

The company specializes in the fitting out and refurbishment of commercial property. It has a very experienced workshop from which it can efficiently prefabricate the structures required for projects using the skill and craftsmanship using modern but standard woodworking machinery, thus allowing for the most efficient manner in which to build.

The downturn in the economy of the construction industry started in 1989. Du Boulay Construction Limited has been able to maintain its order book as commercial businesses have continued to refurbish as opposed to building new property.

The company has a wide network of contact and works closely with architects and designers who provide the design capability for projects.

The company has completed contracts throughout the United Kingdom and in Europe.

The two founding directors were joined in 1984 by Michael Reed who has acted as Contracts Director.

The Equity of the company is as follows:

David Budd   37.5%
David du Boulay   42.5%
Michael Reed   20%

4. History

a) Background

The Company historically grew up in the area of shopfitting and refurbishment of public houses. The fall in the activity of the retail sector meant that activity had to be sought in commercial and office premises. This has resulted in a broad base of contract opportunities.

b) Past results

The trading results of the past five years are (£'000):

Year ended 31 December:

	1986	1987	1988	1989	1990[1]
Sales	740.3	1,121.3	1,363.8	2,145.9	3,568.0
Gross profit	137.4	202.5	248.2	359.2	487.8
GP %	18.6	18.1	18.2	16.7	13.7
Overheads	130.9	148.2	190.1	253.5	414.5
Interest paid	5.5	7.0	9.3	22.8	47.5
Pre-tax profit	1.1	47.4	48.7	83.3	28.1

[1]Note: 15 months to 31 March 1990

An extraordinary item of £191,194 in 1987 turned the net pre-tax operating profit into a loss for the year of £127,526 (after tax repayments)

c) Analysis of trends

Du Boulay Construction have averaged a 22% growth in the last three years. The growth in the shop-fitting industry was about 15%. It can therefore be seen that Du Boulay Construction outperformed the industry. In the general economic climate of today, fierce competition has led to a fall in prices and, although control of site costs is in evidence, there is a natural decline in gross margins.

It should be noted that in 1987, the Company suffered a bad debt which resulted in an extraordinary item of £191,194 appearing in the accounts. This produced a major cash crisis for the Company which was not helped by the simultaneous Stock Market crash when companies abandoned their plans for construction and refurbishment.

The combination of a strong relationship with the Company's bankers and a substantial injection of cash from the Directors kept the Company going so that it could trade itself out of the crisis. Controls were immediately put in place to ensure that this would not happen again.

5   The Market

Du Boulay's market is industry-wide, both in the UK and in Continental Europe.

The client base is mixed and includes brewers, restaurants, wine bars, shops and offices.

Competition is keen, and small and large firms alike are settling for low tenders in the hope of riding this recession.

The company has sought the opportunity to expand into Europe and with the advent of '1992' has gained experience in France where it has refurbished five Oddbins shops in Paris and created two English pubs in two hotels. The company has just completed its third English public house. The company is currently involved in the fitting out of the EuroDisneyland site – just east of Paris – due for completion in April 1992.

It is important for Du Boulay to identify, therefore, companies that are expanding into Europe. As the economy is expected to recover in the second half of 1991, the Company is looking for success in its identification of such corporations which will begin to invest once again with new confidence.

b) Market size

The market size for shopfitting is in excess of £2.5 billion. In the leisure industry the capital expenditure for hotels, pubs, restaurants and clubs is over £1,000 million.

The size is not expected to grow whilst the recession is still in evidence and whilst consumer spending is down. The poll tax and the uniform business rate are also having an effect on the industry and potential growth.

As mentioned before the industry is facing increased competition which will result in some companies failing and is seeking the ability to take opportunities to take a larger share of the dwindling market. However, if the Company is to be successful in this, it will be necessary to continue to keep tight project cost controls.

c) Marketing promotion

There is no advertising or promotional budget. Historically this has not be necessary as the main selling effort has been to architects, the first point of contact.

The company has, however, employed a sales manager who has been critical in winning contracts over the past few months.

6. Manufacturing

One of the company's strengths is that it has its own joinery workshop which has the capability to produce all the joinery requirements for each project. This unit employs skilled joiners.

The in-house joinery facility is important for maintaining high standards of quality and flexibility on each project. By having this under their own control, quality standards can be monitored more effectively.

All timber and other joinery requirements are ordered through the buyer. Stocks are kept to a minimum and these consist mainly of softwood, hardwood and consumables.

b) Material costs

Two factors influence material costs – buying prices and material usage efficiency. It is recognized that the directors have final responsibility for approving purchase prices. Material requirements on site are all routed through the buying department. No site manager is permitted to order materials directly.

Control of site purchases and usage is achieved by reference to the materials budget for that project which the site manager must work within. The buyer monitors site expenditure against budget and is therefore able to control material costs for each project.

7. Personnel

The key personnel are:

a) David du Boulay (Managing Director)

Eighteen years of hands-on experience in project management, estimating and client liaison. Specializes in Victoriana and the Concept Public Houses, having been involved in the design and creation of many.

b) David Budd (Finance Director)

Full-time Finance Director, responsible for overseeing the full accounting function, provision of management information and strategic financial planning. Fully computer literate and responsible for the streamlining of contract details.

c) Michael Reed (Contracts Director)

Four years hands-on experience working on site as a foreman overseeing the construction of a variety of contracts of differing scales and concepts. Then seven years experience in project management and estimation both in Europe and the United Kingdom. Extensive experience in dealing with the technicalities of working abroad.

d) William Thomas BSc (1st Class Hons) Marine Studies (Production Manager)

Controlling all operational details of contracts including the procurement and management of materials and liaison with subcontractors and clients as office based site information centre.

e) Kevin Mulvaney (Business Development Manager)

Specialized in the interiors market for the past five years. Has recently joined the company to take responsibility for the development and implementation of the Du Boulay marketing strategy.

8. Direction of the market

It has been difficult for the industry to see when the recession will 'bottom out'. It will happen that more companies will fail and the Company will be in a position to take a greater share of the market.

The market itself is not likely to develop in the UK for some time. It is the longer-term desire of the Directors to undertake speculative property development. At the present time resources do not permit them to do this. The Directors realize that they will have to wait for the upturn in the market.

9. Strategy and Plans

The objective of the Business Plan is to examine the undoubted strengths of the Company and where they may be exploited, and the factors that may materially improve the performance of the business, and to identify appropriate strategies that may be supported from the resources available.

The various strengths and weaknesses of the company are summarized below.

Strengths

i   A track record of demonstrated expertise to manage significant refurbishment contracts in the UK and in Europe to the highest-quality standards of the industry.

ii   A reputation within the industry that regularly leads to repeat contracts.

iii   An in-house capability to handle the manufacture of specialist joinery.

iv   An ability to generate an increasing sales volume that outstrips the industry's growth norm.

v   An extremely good relationship with bankers arising from good financial forecasting and controls leading to a readiness to provide needed working capital.

vi   A well-balanced management team and staff that has a sense of purpose and high level of motivation.

vii   A Board of Directors that is aware of the need to continually examine the Company's resources and skills and to take necessary action to minimize these.

viii   A spread of business across most commercial/industrial sectors, which ensures that it is not dependent on any one sector.

Weaknesses

i   Under-capitalization of the business, resulting from a significant bad debt.

ii   A falling gross profit percentage.

iii   An inadequate net margin on sales turnover.

iv   A poor liquidity ratio with current liabilities exceeding current assets.

v A need for tighter control of site costs and paperwork prepared by the site foreman.

vi Lack of sales management and a sales team.

vii The lack of in-house design skills.

Objectives

In the knowledge of its strengths and weaknesses the Directors have set the following objectives over the next five years:

i To remain a private company based in south west London.
ii To develop the business into operating subsidiaries with the ability to offer key management shareholding and directorships in the relevant subsidiary.

Initial ideas for subsidiaries are:

- joinery manufacture
- new build projects
- refurbishment work
- property development
- small works department
- design

iii To attain contracts in excess of £500,000.

iv To increase the size of the client base to include the EC as well as the UK.

The Opportunities

Larger contracts are now achievable given the new financial base and management team.

The policy of Wandsworth Council to encourage the use of local contractors for refurbishment work within the Borough under grant-aid schemes.

The advent of '1992' and the EC market.

The Threats

Against these opportunities are certain factors that could pose threats to the Company.

The recession taking longer to 'bottom out'

A liquidity crisis arising from a larger bad debt problem or through clients taking extended credit.

Competition from EC companies

Fierce competition from both local and national low-cost builders seeking new markets as their traditional markets have collapsed during the recession.

Conclusion

The Company has an established reputation for quality work and for a professional management approach.

Financial and other information systems are good, giving the Board the ability to monitor every part of the operation.

The weakness of cost-control on site is being addressed to ensure that projects are kept within budget so that targeted gross margins are achieved.

The recruitment of a Business Development Manager has materially contributed to the achievement of the successful tendering for contracts in the difficult economic climate.

The Company's administrative team and the consequent overhead costs can only be justified on the basis of forecast sales turnover being achieved. This is important to ensure that the Company achieves a level of profitability to build up its own reserves and to reduce its dependence on bank borrowing. In addition it is to enable the present well-motivated and competent team to be retained.

The aspirations of the staff are high and given the anticipated profitable growth they have the opportunity of growing with the business.

The Company has the possibility of an exciting time ahead for everyone involved in the Company, giving the opportunity of giving key managers the possibility of an equity stake in the business and a participation in policy-making decisions.

DE BOULAY CONSTRUCTION LIMITED BUSINESS PLAN
PROFIT AND LOSS ACCOUNT (UNAUDITED)
FOR THE PERIOD ENDED 31 MARCH 1991

	Twelve months 31 March 1991 [£]	Fifteen months 31 March 1990 [£]
TURNOVER	2,199,640	3,568,000
COST OF SALES	(1,883,566)	(3,080,167)
GROSS PROFIT	316,074	487,833
Administrative expenses	(259,005)	(300,648)
Establishment costs	(77,962)	(113,820)
OPERATING PROFIT (LOSS)	(20,893)	73,363
Interest receivable	–	2,262
Interest payable and similar charges	(80,942)	(47,542)
Write-off of investments	(451)	–
Profit (Loss) on ordinary activities before taxation	(102,286)	28,084
TAXATION ON COSTS ON ORDINARY ACTIVITIES	–	(14,895)
PROFIT (LOSS) ON ORDINARY ACTIVITIES AFTER TAXATION	(102,286)	13,188
RETAINED PROFIT/(LOSS) FOR THE PERIOD	(102,286)	13,188
RETAINED DEFICIT BROUGHT FORWARD	(50,360)	(63,548)
RETAINED DEFICIT CARRIED FORWARD	£ (152,646)	£ (50,360)

DE BOULAY CONSTRUCTION LIMITED BUSINESS PLAN
BALANCE SHEET
AS AT 31 MARCH 1991 (UNAUDITED)

	[31 March 1991] [£]	[31 March 1991] [£]	[31 March 1990] [£]	[31 March 1990] [£]
FIXED ASSETS				
Tangible assets		134,776		129,782
CURRENT ASSETS				
Stock and WIP	210,525		15,090	
Debtors	482,564		824,078	
Investments	10,252		10,702	
Cash at bank and in hand	2,012		2,294	
	705,353		852,164	
CREDITORS				
Amounts falling due within one year	(834,550)		(901,080)	
NET CURRENT LIABILITIES		(129,197)		(48,916)
TOTAL ASSETS LESS CURRENT LIABILITIES		5,579		80,866
CREDITORS				
Amounts falling due after more than one year		(148,171)		(121,172)
NET ASSETS		£ (142,592)		£ (40,306)
FINANCED BY:				
CAPITAL RESERVES				
Share capital		10,054		10,054
Profit and loss account		(152,646)		(50,360)
		£ (142,592)		£ (40,306)

DU BOULAY CONSTRUCTION LIMITED
PROJECTED PROFIT & LOSS ACCOUNT
FOR THE SIX MONTHS ENDED
31 JANUARY 1992

	August 1991	September 1991	October 1991	November 1991	December 1991	January 1992	Total
SALES	50,000	110,000	395,000	395,000	150,000	350,000	1,450,000
COST OF SALES							
Purchases	44,450	97,790	351,155	351,155	133,350	311,150	1,289,050
Production salaries							0
GROSS PROFIT	5,550	12,210	43,845	43,845	16,650	38,850	160,950
GROSS PROFIT PER CENT	11%	11%	11%	11%	11%	11%	11%
OVERHEADS							
Cash payments	20,869	21,697	22,140	-22,379	23,218	22,528	132,831
Depreciation	3,104	2,176	2,135	2,096	2,056	2,017	13,584
	23,973	23,873	24,275	24,475	25,274	24,545	146,415
OPERATING PROFIT	-18,423	-11,663	-19,570	-19,370	-8,264	-14,305	-14,535
TAXATION							0
NET PROFIT	-18,423	-11,663	-19,570	-19,370	-8,624	-14,305	-14,305

DU BOULAY CONSTRUCTION LIMITED
PROJECTED OVERHEADS
FOR THE SIX MONTHS ENDED
31 JANUARY 1992

	August 1991	September 1991	October 1991	November 1991	December 1991	January 1992	Total
ADMINISTRATION							
Rent & rates	3,602	3,602	3,602	3,602	3,602	3,602	21,612
Light & heat	412	412	412	412	412	412	2,472
Insurance	1,260	1,260	1,260	1,260	1,260	1,260	7,560
Cleaning	50	50	50	50	50	50	300
Motor expenses	650	650	650	650	650	650	3,900
Travel	150	150	150	150	150	150	900
Directors pension	242	242	242	242	242	242	1,452
Directors remuneration	600	600	600	600	600	600	3,600
Wages & salaries	9,250	9,250	9,250	9,250	9,250	9,250	55,500
National Insurance	962	962	962	962	962	962	5,772
Audit & accountancy	225	225	225	225	225	225	1,350
Telephone	853	853	853	853	853	853	5,118
Prin.post.stat.	1,039	1,039	1,039	1,039	1,039	1,039	6,234
Sundry expenses	795	795	795	795	795	795	4,770
	20,090	20,090	20,090	20,090	20,090	20,090	120,540
SELLING & DISTRIBUTION							
Marketing	83	83	83	83	83	83	498
	83	83	83	83	83	83	498
FINANCIAL							
Bank interest 14.50%	696	1,524	1,967	2,206	3,045	2,355	11,793
	696	1,524	1,967	2,206	3,045	2,355	11,793
TOTAL	20,869	21,697	22,140	22,379	23,218	22,528	132,831

170

DU BOULAY CONSTRUCTION LIMITED
PROJECTED CASH FLOW
FOR THE SIX MONTHS ENDED
31 JANUARY 1992

	August 1991	September 1991	October 1991	November 1991	December 1991	January 1992	Total
RECEIPTS							
From debtors	54,991	260,385	269,549	349,035	406,139	312,550	1,652,649
	54,991	260,385	269,549	349,035	406,139	312,550	1,652,649
PAYMENTS							
To creditors	92,403	263,643	261,857	378,863	314,678	303,188	1,614,632
Overheads	20,869	21,697	22,140	22,379	23,218	22,528	132,831
Prepayments/(Accruals)	−734	0	0	0	0	0	−734
VAT							
On overheads	2,809	2,809	2,809	2,809	2,809	2,809	16,854
Returns	0	0	0	2,354	0	0	2,354
HP CAPITAL AND LOAN REPAYMENTS	4,180	4,470	2,500	2,200	3,878	9,704	26,932
OTHER	4,000	4,450	0	9,900	4,450	4,450	27,250
	123,527	297,069	289,306	418,505	349,033	342,679	1,820,119
Net movement	−68,536	−36,684	−19,757	−69,470	57,106	−30,129	−167,470
Balance b/f	−57,561	−126,097	−162,781	−182,538	−252,008	−194,902	−57,561
Balance c/f	−126,097	−162,781	−182,538	−252,008	−194,902	−225,031	−225,031

171

DU BOULAY CONSTRUCTION LIMITED
PROJECTED BALANCE SHEET
FOR THE SIX MONTHS ENDED
31 JANUARY 1992

	Opening Balance	August 1991	September 1991	October 1991	November 1991	December 1991	January 1992
FIXED ASSETS							
Cost	298,233	298,233	298,233	298,233	298,233	298,233	298,233
Depreciation	−171,227	−174,331	−176,507	−178,642	−181,738	−183,749	−184,811
	127,006	123,902	121,726	119,591	117,495	115,439	113,422
CURRENT ASSETS							
Stocks	107,977	107,977	107,977	107,977	107,977	107,977	107,977
Debtors	491,162	494,921	363,786	558,362	673,452	443,563	542,263
Prepayments/(accruals)	734	0	0	0	0	0	0
Bank & cash	0	0	0	0	0	0	0
Other	33,916	33,916	33,916	33,916	33,916	33,916	33,916
	663,789	636,814	505,679	700,255	815,345	585,456	684,156
CURRENT LIABILITIES							
Overdraft	−57,561	−126,097	−162,781	−182,538	−252,008	−194,902	−225,031
Trade creditors	−563,790	−523,616	−374,876	−525,626	−559,370	−401,378	−463,791
VAT	0	1,838	2,510	−2,354	−4,864	−4,969	−8,959
HP and loans	−46,428	−42,248	−37,778	−35,278	−33,078	−29,200	−19,496
Other	−83,300	−79,300	−74,850	−74,850	−64,950	−60,500	−56,050
Sundry creditors	−111,407	−111,407	−111,407	−111,407	−111,407	−111,407	−111,407
	−862,486	−880,830	−759,182	−932,053	−1,025,677	−802,356	−884,734
NET ASSETS	−101,691	−120,114	−131,777	−112,207	−92,837	−101,461	−87,156
SHARE CAPITAL	10,054	10,054	10,054	10,054	10,054	10,054	10,054
RETAINED RESERVES							
Opening	−111,745	−111,745	−130,168	−141,831	−122,261	−102,891	−111,515
Profit for month		−18,423	−11,663	−19,570	−19,370	−8,264	−14,305
less: Distributions		0	0	0	0	0	0
	−111,745	−130,168	−141,831	−122,261	−102,891	−111,515	−97,210
	−101,691	−120,114	−131,777	−112,207	−92,837	−101,461	−87,156

DU BOULAY CONSTRUCTION LIMITED
NOTES TO THE PROJECTIONS
FOR THE SIX MONTHS ENDED
31 JANUARY 1992

1. DEBTORS

	August 1991	September 1991	October 1991	November 1991	December 1991	January 1992	Total
B/f	491,162	494,921	363,786	558,362	673,452	443,563	491,162
Sales	50,000	110,000	395,000	395,000	150,000	350,000	1,450,000
VAT	8,750	19,250	69,125	69,125	26,250	61,250	253,750
Cash received	−54,991	−260,385	−269,549	−349,035	−406,139	−312,550	−1,652,649
C/f	494,921	363,786	558,362	673,452	443,563	542,263	542,263

REPAYMENT PROFILE

	Opening Balance	August 1991 Sales	September 1991 Sales	October 1991 Sales	November 1991 Sales	December 1991 Sales	January 1992 Sales
Month 0	10%	10%	10%	10%	10%	10%	10%
Month 1	45%	45%	45%	45%	45%	45%	45%
Month 2	30%	30%	30%	30%	30%	30%	30%
Month 3	10%	10%	10%	10%	10%	10%	10%
Month 4	5%	5%	5%	5%	5%	5%	5%
Total	100%	100%	100%	100%	100%	100%	100%

173

NOTES TO THE PROJECTIONS (Cont.)

2. CREDITORS

	August 1991	September 1991	October 1991	November 1991	December 1991	January 1992	August 1991
B/f	563,790	523,616	374,876	525,626	559,370	401,378	563,790
Purchases	44,450	97,790	351,155	351,155	133,350	311,150	1,289,050
VAT	7,779	17,113	61,452	61,452	23,336	54,451	225,583
Cash paid	−92,403	−263,643	−261,857	−378,863	−314,678	−303,188	−1,614,632
C/f	523,616	374,876	525,626	559,370	401,378	463,791	463,791

REPAYMENT PROFILE

	Opening Balance	August 1991 Purchases	September 1991 Purchases	October 1991 Purchases	November 1991 Purchases	December 1991 Purchases	January 1992 Purchases
Month 0	15%	15%	15%	15%	15%	15%	15%
Month 1	40%	40%	40%	40%	40%	40%	40%
Month 2	25%	25%	25%	25%	25%	25%	25%
Month 3	20%	20%	20%	20%	20%	20%	20%
Month 4	0%	0%	0%	0%	0%	0%	0%
Total	100%	100%	100%	100%	100%	100%	100%

NOTES TO THE PROJECTIONS (Cont.)

3. VALUE ADDED TAX

	August 1991	September 1991	October 1991	November 1991	December 1991	January 1992	Total
B/f	0	−1,838	−2,510	2,354	4,864	4,969	0
Sales	8,750	19,250	69,125	69,125	26,250	61,250	253,750
Purchases	−7,779	−17,113	−61,452	−61,452	−23,336	−54,451	−225,583
Overheads	−2,809	−2,809	−2,809	−2,809	−2,809	−2,809	−16,854
VAT payments				−2,353			−2,354
C/f	−1,838	−2,510	2,354	4,864	4,969	8,959	8,959

4. REPAYMENTS

	Opening Balance	August 1991	September 1991	October 1991	November 1991	December 1991	January 1992
Rent							
Insurance							
Other	28,402	0	0	0	0	0	0
Total	28,402	0	0	0	0	0	0

5. ACCRUALS

	Opening Balance	August 1991	September 1991	October 1991	November 1991	December 1991	January 1992
Accruals	27,668	0	0	0	0	0	0
	27,668	0	0	0	0	0	0

NOTES TO THE PROJECTIONS (Cont.)

6. STOCKS & WIP

	August 1991	September 1991	October 1991	November 1991	December 1991	January 1992	Total
B/f	107,977	107,977	107,977	107,977	107,977	107,977	107,977
Purchases	44,450	97,790	351,155	351,155	133,350	311,150	1,289,050
Cost of sales	−44,450	−97,790	−351,155	−351,155	−133,350	−311,150	−1,289,050
C/f	107,977	107,977	107,977	107,977	107,977	107,977	107,977

NOTES TO THE PROJECTIONS (Cont.)

7. FIXED ASSETS

	August 1991	September 1991	October 1991	November 1991	December 1991	January 1992	Total
PLANT & EQUIPMENT							
Cost:							
B/f	38,653	38,653	38,653	38,653	38,653	38,653	38,653
Additions	0	0	0	0	0	0	0
Disposals							0
C/f	38,653	38,653	38,653	38,653	38,653	38,653	38,653
Depreciation:	25%	25%	25%	25%	25%	25%	25%
B/f	28,260	28,476	28,688	28,896	29,099	29,298	28,260
Charge	216	212	208	203	199	195	1,233
Disposals							0
C/f	28,476	28,688	28,896	29,099	29,298	29,493	29,493
Net book value	10,177	9,965	9,757	9,554	9,355	9,160	9,160
FURNITURE & FITTINGS							
Cost:							
B/f	32,161	32,161	32,161	32,161	32,161	32,161	32,161
Additions	0	0	0	0	0	0	0
Disposals							0
C/f	32,161	32,161	32,161	32,161	32,161	32,161	32,161
Depreciation:	20%	20%	20%	20%	20%	20%	25%
B/f	17,973	18,212	18,444	18,673	18,898	19,119	17,973
Charge	239	232	229	225	221	217	1,363
Disposals							0
C/f	18,212	18,444	18,673	18,898	19,119	19,336	19,336
Net book value	13,949	13,717	13,488	13,263	13,042	12,825	12,825

NOTES TO THE PROJECTIONS (Cont.)

MOTOR VEHICLES

Cost:							
B/f	108,139	108,139	108,139	108,139	108,139	108,139	108,139
Additions	0	0	0	0	0	0	0
Disposals							
C/f	108,139	108,139	108,139	108,139	108,139	108,139	108,139
Depreciation:	25%	27%	27%	27%	27%	27%	27%
B/f	57,690	63,909	62,891	61,849	60,784	59,694	57,690
Charge	7,214	995	1,018	1,042	1,065	1,090	2,004
Disposals	0						
C/f	64,904	64,904	63,909	62,891	61,849	60,784	59,694
Net book value	43,235	43,235	44,230	45,248	46,290	47,355	48,445

OTHER ASSETS

Cost:							
B/f	119,280	119,280	119,280	119,280	119,280	119,280	119,280
Additions	0	0	0	0	0	0	0
Disposals							
C/f	119,280	119,280	119,280	119,280	119,280	119,280	119,280
Depreciation:	25%	15%	15%	15%	15%	15%	15%
B/f	67,304	70,468	69,850	69,224	68,591	67,949	67,304
Charge	3,774	610	618	626	633	642	645
Disposals	0						
C/f	71,078	71,078	70,468	69,850	69,224	68,591	67,949
Net book value	48,202	48,202	48,812	49,430	50,056	50,689	51,331

TOTAL

COST	298,233	298,233	298,233	298,233	298,233	298,233	298,233
DEPRECIATION	174,331	184,811	182,794	180,738	178,642	176,507	174,331
NET BOOK VALUE	123,902	113,422	115,439	117,495	119,591	121,726	123,902